THRIVE IN THE YEAR OF THE RABBIT

Chinese Zodiac Horoscope 2023

Linda Dearsley

BENNION
KEARNY

Published in 2022 by Bennion Kearny

ISBN: 978-0-9570511-6-4

CHAPTER 1: SUCCESS IN THE YEAR OF THE RABBIT

And now, for something completely different! Welcome to the brand new – and hopefully cuddly – Year of the Black Rabbit.

Because let's face it, whatever the Tiger Year of 2022 (recently passed), had going for it – cuddly it was not. So just when you thought you couldn't take any more drama – along comes the reassuring Rabbit.

The Year of the Rabbit that is, of course, bouncing into the world on January 22nd 2023, like a one-creature, bob-tailed, peace-keeping force, spreading tolerance and harmony in all directions. What's more, this soothing bunny intends to dig in, exuding calming vibes right up to February 9th 2024, when the Dragon takes over.

As far as many of us are concerned, a Rabbit year can only come as a relief.

Goodbye Endless Crisis

By now, most of us are finding the full-on, non-stop, often confrontational atmosphere of the turbulent Tiger year that was 2022 downright exhausting.

Tiger years are renowned for getting things moving, activating change, breaking down barriers, and highlighting injustices. That's their job. And Tiger doesn't do slow and steady. Tiger tends to dive straight in, seize the situation by the throat, and it won't let go till the job's done.

This may well be an efficient approach, but after 12 months of constant, sudden, and often shocking change, even the most extrovert and hardy of signs could do with a pause to get their breath back.

So, if this year you're hoping for a spell of tranquillity, some time to adjust and develop your ideas, to think creatively, and maybe even enjoy yourself a little along the way, 2023 could be the year you've been waiting for.

Did Something Go Wrong in 2022?

Probably not. Strange as it may seem, after the whole world more or less ground to a halt for nearly the entire two years that were 2020 and 2021 because of COVID and all its ramifications, it was going to take a very powerful energy to get things moving again.

So right on cue, out sprang the Tiger – an astrological super-force honed for just such dynamic action. Tiger's energy can be aggressive, of course, which might explain the war in Ukraine, but it's ultimately aimed at improving situations by changing what needs to be changed – even if the methods do seem unnecessarily drastic at the time. When a Tiger year comes to an end, no one can claim things are just the same as they were at the beginning. Tiger years tend to be remembered.

Hop Forward the Gentle Rabbit

It's no accident a Rabbit Year always follows a Tiger Year in the Chinese tradition. Ancient Chinese wisdom asserts that all creation strives for balance, as in night and day, hot and cold, wet and dry, and so on. You have to have one to appreciate the other. Therefore, a hyper-energetic year such as 2022 must be followed by a more restful antidote.

Which is where the soft-pawed Rabbit comes in. Unlikely as it seems, Tiger and Rabbit years always come as a pair – two sides of the same coin endlessly playing out a celestial game of bad cop/good cop.

So, after the tough, cruel-to-be-kind events of 2022, the world is ready for Rabbit's balancing fluffiness in 2023.

Lucky Rabbit Years

The other great thing about the Chinese astrological Rabbit is that it symbolises good luck. And not just in China. For centuries, Rabbits have been associated with good luck in many cultures. In fact, until recently, people in the west would carry a rabbit's foot in their pocket or on a key-ring as a lucky charm.

And as well as being lucky, the Chinese astrological Rabbit is regarded as one of the happiest signs of the zodiac.

In parts of China, buns baked in the shape of carefree rabbits used to be eaten at weddings, particularly by the bride, to ensure the couple were blessed with healthy children and the marriage was prosperous.

To this day, the Rabbit represents youth and optimism. So, in 2023, the interests of children and babies are likely to be particularly important; an atmosphere of peace and diplomacy will be encouraged and rewarded, while ruthless, uncivilised, or boorish behaviour is likely to backfire on the perpetrator.

The Healing Power of Water

But why should we be treated specifically to a Black Rabbit in 2023, you might be wondering. Particularly as this comes straight after the Year of the Black Tiger. What is it with the colour black?

Well, in Chinese tradition, black is the colour that represents water. As well as being ruled by a zodiac animal, each pair of years is believed to be ruled by an element too.

The element sweeps in, in its strongest, most powerful form in year one; in the following year, it works its way out in its quieter, softer guise. All in balance, of course... the ancient Chinese way.

So, the Black Water Tiger brought us water in its most forceful incarnation; the roaring torrent that can either power a hydro-electric dam and benefit thousands, or morph into a raging flood destroying everything in its path – which might explain the unprecedented floods in Pakistan last year.

Fortunately, we're finally done with such extremes. They disappeared with Tiger. Now the Black Water Rabbit brings H_2O in its more agreeable form; think silvery streams sliding beneath willows, or soft spring rains that make the flowers grow.

Yes, the Black Rabbit of 2023 is aiming to sprinkle the healing energies of water across the whole year.

Activate Your Rabbit Luck

So, what will the Year of the Black Rabbit bring to you? We're all hoping for better times ahead, but will the Rabbit's famous good fortune find its way to you, or should you be out there trying to attract its attention? Worse, could you inadvertently do something to scare the nervous bunny away, so it bypasses you altogether?

According to Chinese astrology, *it's up to you*. No matter what your sign, you get to choose how you're going to respond to the Rabbit year – and the choices you make will shape your destiny in 2023. Play it clever, and you can charm shy Rabbit into snuggling close all year, showering you with bunny blessings. Get it wrong, and Rabbit will turn timid and hop away, taking all the goodies with him.

Yet, the secret to winning the Rabbit's trust is deceptively simple. Once you understand the nature of the creature, and how it interacts with your particular sign, the path becomes clear. As soon as you know what you're dealing with, you can formulate a fool-proof plan!

Life is what happens when you're making other plans...

The famous quote from a lyric on John Lennon's *Double Fantasy* album is just as true today as it was back in 1980 when the album was released. Actually, John may have borrowed those words of wisdom from a quote in the *Reader's Digest* of 1957. But hey, what does it matter who said it first?

He was talking, of course, about the underhand way unforeseen events have, of sneaking up on us when we least expect them and throwing our careful plans into total disarray or knocking us off course altogether.

Yet this annoying syndrome is less likely to plague followers of Chinese astrology. Very few of us possess an operational crystal ball, of course. The future is always a mystery, unless you're a fully paid-up professional psychic.

But in Chinese astrology, no year *ever arrives as a completely unguessable blank*. As the New Year dawns, according to Chinese lore, a totally different energy is unleashed on the world. It comes in the form of a zodiac character bristling with its own unique 'personality' – fully-formed and ready to reshape the coming months to its own satisfaction.

So, by understanding those zodiac personalities, by studying the effect the new energy will have, you can work out the kind of year we have in store and how best to handle it.

You'd know that actions that might have led to chaos when meticulous Ox is in charge could prove an exhilarating roller-coaster ride in a daring Dragon year. Or that a bold, take-no-prisoners escapade could lead to fame and fortune when Tiger's at the helm, but try that when stickler-for-the-rules Dog is judge and jury, and you'll find yourself locked up.

This priceless advance information could be the crucial difference between success and failure.

Meet the Black Rabbit – diplomat extraordinaire

The other thing to bear in mind is that not every zodiac Rabbit is the same. Like all the creatures in Chinese astrology, the Rabbit comes in five different varieties – think of them as breeds. All Rabbits, of course, are endowed with basic Rabbit traits, but each sports pelts of different hues and displays slightly different personalities.

As well as the Black Water Rabbit, there's also the Red Fire Rabbit, the Green Wood Rabbit, the Brown Earth Rabbit, and the White or Gold Metal Rabbit, and every twelve years, each one gets a turn to take charge.

2023 belongs to the Black Water Rabbit, as mentioned, and while all Rabbits strive for harmony and compromise, the Black Rabbit is the master mediator of them all.

This is because water is the element believed to symbolise communication, emotion, and flexibility – blessings that make Black Rabbit the sweet-talking, smoothest operator of the clan.

So, as 2023 opens, it's obvious Tiger has ruffled a great many feathers, collateral damage has been done, and misunderstandings abound.

But don't expect the Rabbit to undo all Tiger's changes. Rabbit's job is to modify and refine, sand off the rough edges, affect any necessary repairs, and generally render Tiger's revolution acceptable, even welcome, to all.

But it's been 60 years since the last Black Rabbit hopped quietly out to savour the new era; over half a century of patient preparation. So, to get an insight into what kind of developments Black Rabbit might bring us in 2023, we can take a look at what happened when his grandpa – the Black Rabbit of 1963 – took charge.

Digging the Far-Out Black Rabbit of 1963

First light in Britain on the morning of January 25th 1963, filtered blearily out onto sparkling snowdrifts in the countryside and greying-mountains of frozen slush in the towns. It was the coldest winter of the century, and as the Black Rabbit peeked out to survey the chill scene, he could have been forgiven for turning tail and leaving the job to Tiger, to extend the big cat stay.

Unusually cold weather was also causing havoc in the USA, the Far East, and the rest of Europe – a sizeable chunk of the entire world. To be fair to the Rabbit of '63, the ferocious freeze began under Tiger's watch and it was left to Rabbit to initiate the thaw, which took some time.

In the case of the UK, it was early March before the snow finally melted away. Intriguingly, March is the Rabbit's special month when Rabbit powers could be at their strongest. Even more intriguingly, there was actually a brief thaw on January 25th – the day the Rabbit arrived – but the cold was still so brutal, Rabbit's energies weren't yet powerful enough to break the freeze.

A Tragedy that Shook the Globe

Yet, as things turned out, it wasn't the weather that was destined to make 1963 famous for all the wrong reasons. The Black Rabbit's reign was to be marred by an event that shocked and horrified the world and which, in years to come, was to obscure almost everything else that happened during those 12 months.

For 1963 was the year the adored young President of the USA, John F Kennedy, was assassinated; shot as he motored through the cheering crowds of Dallas, Texas, in an open-top car, beside his glamorous wife, Jackie.

That was in November 1963, towards the end of the Rabbit rule and chances are, according to various theories, the crime was probably planned long before that date. It's possible the seeds of the tragedy were sown during the previous Tiger year.

Nevertheless, it was left to Rabbit energy to re-establish calm, pick up the pieces, and smooth the way for vice president Lyndon Johnson to take over the White House.

All Change at the Top

Oddly, in the same year, there was also a change of leader in Britain, and just as in the USA, the leader was changed without a public election.

Long-term British Prime Minister, Harold 'Supermac' Macmillan, resigned in October 1963, citing 'health reasons'. Many believed this a convenient excuse.

Macmillan's reputation had been irretrievably damaged, it was thought, by the recent Profumo sex scandal involving a government minister and two party girls – Christine Keeler and her friend Mandy Rice Davies. So Macmillan diplomatically resigned and his colleague Alec Douglas Home, formerly the Foreign Secretary, replaced him.

Fab to be a Teen

Dimmed now by the seismic events that were to come in the USA, at the time, 1963 seemed to be the year that youthful, optimistic Rabbit energy was sweeping the world.

The Beatles, from Liverpool – nicknamed by the press as 'the lovable mop-tops' owing to their groundbreaking hair-cuts (allegedly invented by inverting a pudding bowl over their shaggy locks and trimming around it) – were the most exciting phenomenon that Britain and later the world, had ever seen. In 1963, hit after Fab Four hit raced up the charts, inspiring a new kind of fan worship the older generation found disturbing.

Uncontrollable young girls drowned out the music at Beatle concerts with hysterical screaming; they collapsed, overcome, in the aisles and made demented assaults on the stage. They camped for days around any building the Fab Four were believed to have entered, ambushed any car suspected of carrying their idols, and chased them down the streets should they be foolhardy enough to step outside.

By autumn, the scenes of mass hysteria that accompanied the Liverpool lads' every move was dubbed 'Beatlemania'. The world had seen nothing like it.

London Swings

The same year, a men's fashion shop – Lord John – opened in Carnaby Street, a tiny backwater in central London. Cranks (regarded by older diners as an eccentric, peasant-style, vegetarian restaurant) had already set up shop there, and young people were soon flocking to sample the novel wares.

The Rolling Stones, the Kinks, and every other band aspiring to be 'trendy' began gravitating to Lord John for groovy threads. Other fashion boutiques rapidly moved in, and soon Carnaby Street had become the epicentre of a youth culture that was to change the world. London was beginning to swing.

By the end of the year, children no longer wanted to be train-drivers and nurses when they grew up; they wanted to be pop stars!

Giving Peace A Chance

As the year progressed, the peaceful, diplomatic energy of the Rabbit began to work its magic. The United States signed a Partial Nuclear Test Ban Treaty, which forbade all nuclear weapon testing that was not conducted underground. The treaty was to be credited for slowing down the world's arms race for years to come.

And, by August, the famous 'hotline' between the Pentagon and the Kremlin was set up – allowing the two Superpower presidents to speak to each other instantly for the first time, in the hope of avoiding the kind of misunderstandings that could lead to World War III.

Sit-ins and Protest Rallies

Although the Rabbit would always prefer compromise and discussion to violent confrontation, this is not a 'walk-all-over-me' kind of energy. Consequently, 1963 was soon vibrating to the sound of protesting youth. In the West, hardly a week went by without some sort of demonstration or march. In the USA, the American civil rights movement gathered ever-increasing momentum; there were sit-ins at universities, defiance in segregated restaurants, and 1963 was the year when Martin Luther King made his legendary 'I have a dream' speech on the steps of the Lincoln Memorial in Washington, during a march for Jobs and Freedom.

Bring on the Entertainment

The water element was in full flow in 1963, enhancing communication in all directions. Under this invigorating influence, all forms of entertainment flourished. TV viewers revelled in good-humoured, family-oriented shows: *The Beverley Hillbillies*, *The Lucy Show*, the *Dick Van Dyke Show*, and *Steptoe and Son*, while the eerie new children's sci-fi series *Dr Who* thrilled-while-it-delightfully-terrified the under twelves, and rapidly became essential viewing.

At the cinema, classics such as Hitchcock's *The Birds*, *The Great Escape*, *From Russia with Love*, and *The Pink Panther* got their first showings, while in publishing, John Le Carré's *The Spy Who Came in from the Cold* made its debut, as did Maurice Sendak's children's story *Where the Wild Things Are* – both still being enjoyed to this day.

Never Underestimate Water Power

Yet, even under the benevolent influence of the Rabbit, the water element can be dangerously unpredictable. The year had begun with a sensational display of water in its frozen form, to be known ever afterwards as 'The Big Freeze', but once spring had warmed the world, the element seemed to have slipped back into its docile, nurturing guise.

Until October 1963 came around, that was! Suddenly, days of heavy rain began to hammer the Dolomite Mountains in Northern Italy until the ground became so waterlogged that the saturated earth could absorb no more. Late on the night of October 9th, rocks at the top of Monte Toc gave way, causing a landslide that sent half a hillside crashing into the recently completed Vajont Dam, one of the tallest dams in the world.

The 70 mph impact created a wave 300ft high, which rocketed the length of the dam, swept right over the rim at the end, and tore down the gorge below, wiping out the town of Longarone in minutes and roaring on to engulf several more villages along the valley.

Around 2,500 people are believed to have died that night.

The siting of the dam had been controversial. Warnings about the unstable geology of the region had been dismissed in previous years. Perhaps, for a while, it seemed as if the critics had been overcautious – until the second water year in a row arrived and washed away all doubt with a vengeance.

The Cool Black Rabbit of 2023

So, having seen what happened last time Black Rabbit took the wheel, what can we expect from 2023?

Well, should the Tiger of 2022 leave us with a cold, frosty winter, it looks as if it will take the Rabbit a while to warm things up. But once the new energy takes hold, we can expect to see a calming and a cooling on the international scene.

Previous enemies are unlikely to become good friends, but in 2023 they're at least ready to start negotiating. Compromises will be found, and the atmosphere of aggression that was ratcheting up and up last year will begin to dissipate.

Although we lost Queen Elizabeth II in 2022, and the UK also had a new prime minister, we could still see two world leaders unexpectedly depart in 2023 to be replaced with fresh, probably younger faces.

A Passion for Fashion

As we all start to relax under Rabbit's calming vibes in 2023, the influence of the elegant, stylish bobtail will inspire many of us to take a good long look in our wardrobes and decide the whole lot suddenly appears cheap and shabby.

The Rabbit prefers quality over quantity, and that goes for the home environment, too, particularly as the Rabbit regards home as a precious sanctuary.

So, 2023 is likely to see a renaissance in the fashion industry and also in interior design. As those shoddy, cheap-as-chips bargain clothes hit the recycling bin, they're likely to be joined by junk furniture.

Creative businesses that can produce classy-looking clothes and footwear at affordable prices, particularly if they have a youthful twist, will prosper.

And watch out for a new Mary Quant to emerge who will shake up the fashion industry and transform the way we look.

Dinner at Mine

As the isolation caused by the pandemic fades away, Rabbit's gregarious instincts are likely to unleash a huge wave of sociability. Suddenly, we all want to get together, ideally in our own homes.

Yet, just like our wardrobes, the cosy COVID bolthole that was fine when it was just us – hiding from the world – is likely to need some serious smartening up before the guests arrive.

The Rabbit is not particularly known for its enthusiasm for DIY, so many will prefer to leave improvements to the experts; but if budgets are strained, a craze for tasteful upcycling is likely to spread.

Decorators, gardeners, upholsterers, and curtain-makers will flourish, home-handyman businesses won't have enough hours in the day and craftspeople everywhere making unusual and attractive *objets* will find their unique creations flying out the door.

Pleasure and leisure...

2023 marks the second and final year of the water element for nearly a decade – water doesn't return until it swims in with the Water Rat of

2032 – so the urge to communicate will become unstoppable this year. On the international stage, we can look forward to discreet diplomacy behind the scenes, and honeyed words in front of them.

On a national level, social media, public debates, private counselling, and demonstrations of all kinds will become even more enticing than ever.

An intense longing for gatherings and meetings in person rather than online will result in festivals, markets, rallies – anything people-oriented – gaining even more popularity.

Above all, entertainment will blossom. Music, the theatre, TV, film and literature will see an explosion of innovation that – just as in 1963 – is likely to create new stars in every field for years to come.

And, of course, perhaps one of the most dramatic and spectacular performances of all occurs in 2023 – the coronation of King Charles III – the first coronation in Britain for 70 years. A spectacle likely to enthral the world.

Sexy Scandals

No year goes by without its share of scandal, of course. Under the influence of the water element – with such emphasis on communication – much of this year's scandal will centre on communication's dark side… lies and deceit. The truth will come spilling out in 2023, and once it starts, a tiny trickle will turn into an awesome flood.

Expect the culprits to wriggle and evade with lie piling on lie – but the relentless power of water will wear away all excuses.

And this being a Rabbit year, of course, we can expect some of the biggest scandals to involve sex.

Any politician or prominent person in the public eye had better take care to play by the rules because their indiscretions will be revealed.

It was probably no accident that back in 1963, when the last Black Rabbit ruled the year, British Prime Minister Macmillan ended up resigning over a sex scandal which didn't even involve himself!

Mini Breaks All Round

Despite the economists' predictions of financial misery for most of us in 2023, the Rabbit is associated with happy times. It is likely our prospects won't be as dire as many feared.

True, budgets might be stretched, but Rabbit's influence will inspire us to enjoy ourselves with family and friends and swap long, expensive holidays for a well-chosen mini-break or three.

And since it's quality – not quantity – that counts this year, chances are that many will find they actually prefer it that way.

Why is the Year called Rabbit?

According to Chinese folklore, there are many explanations as to why the calendar is divided up the way it is. Perhaps the most popular is the story about the supreme Jade Emperor who lives in heaven. He decided to name each year in honour of a different animal and decreed that a race would be run to decide which animals would be chosen, and the order in which they would appear.

Twelve animals arrived to take part. Actually, in one legend there were 13, and included the cat, at the time a great friend of the rat. But the cat was a sleepy creature and asked the rat to wake him in time for the race and in the excitement (or was it by design?), the rat forgot and dashed off, leaving the cat fast asleep. The cat missed the race and missed out on getting a year dedicated to his name. Which is why cats have hated rats ever since.

Anyway, as they approached the finish line, the 12 competitors found a wide river blocking their route. The powerful Ox, a strong swimmer, plunged straight in, but the tiny Rat begged to be carried across on his back. Kindly Ox agreed, but when they reached the opposite bank, the wily Rat scampered down Ox's body, jumped off his head and shot across the finish line in first place. Which is why the Rat is the first animal of the Chinese zodiac, followed by the Ox.

The muscular Tiger, weighed down by his magnificent coat, arrived in third place, followed by the non-swimming Rabbit who'd found some rocks downstream and hopped neatly from one to another, until it spotted a log floating downstream and jumped on to be carried safely to dry land.

The Emperor was surprised to see the Dragon with his great wings, fly in, in fifth place, instead of the expected first. The Dragon explained that while high up in the sky he saw a village in flames and the people running out of their houses in great distress, so he'd made a detour and employed his rain-making skills (Chinese Dragons can create water as well as fire) to put out the blaze before returning to the race. In some versions of the story, Dragon also adds that as he approached the river he spotted poor little Rabbit clinging perilously to a log, so Dragon gently blew the log across and watched to see Rabbit safely ashore before flying over himself.

In sixth place came the Snake. Clever as the Rat, the Snake had wrapped himself around one of the Horse's hooves and hung on while the Horse swam the river. When the Horse climbed ashore, the Snake slithered off, so startling the Horse that it reared up in alarm, allowing the Snake to slide over the finish line ahead of him.

The Goat, Monkey, and Rooster arrived next at the river. They spotted some driftwood and rope washed up on the shore, so Monkey deftly lashed them together to make a raft and the three of them hopped aboard and floated across. The Goat jumped off first, swiftly followed by Monkey and Rooster. They found they'd beaten the Dog, which was unexpected as the Dog was a good swimmer.

It turned out the Dog so enjoyed the water, he'd hung around playing in the shallows emerging only in time to come eleventh. Last of all came the Pig, not the best of swimmers, and further slowed by his decision to pause for a good meal before exerting himself in the current.

And so the wheel of the zodiac was set forevermore, with the Year of the Rat beginning the cycle, followed by the Ox, Tiger, Rabbit, Dragon, Snake, Horse, Goat, Monkey, Rooster, Dog and Pig.

How to Succeed in 2023

So, since 2023 is the Year of the Rabbit, how will you fare? Does the Rabbit present your astrological animal with opportunities or challenges? As the fable about how the years got their names shows, every one of the astrological animals is resourceful in its own special way. Faced with the daunting prospect of crossing the river, each successfully made it to the other side, even the creatures that could barely swim.

So, whether your year animal gets on easily with the Black Water Rabbit, or whether they have to work at their relationship, you can make 2023 a wonderful year to remember.

Chinese Astrology has been likened to a weather forecast. Once you know whether you'll need your umbrella or your suntan lotion, you can step out with confidence and enjoy the trip.

Find Your Chinese Astrology Sign

To find your Chinese sign, just look up your birth year in the table below.

Important note: if you were born in January or February, check the dates of the New Year very carefully. The Chinese New Year follows the lunar calendar and the beginning and end dates are not fixed, but vary each year. If you were born before mid-February, your animal sign might actually be the sign of the previous year. For example, 1980 was the year of the Monkey, but the Chinese New Year began on February 16, so a person born in January or early February 1980 would belong to the year before – the year of the Goat.

And there's More to it Than That...

In case you're saying to yourself, but surely, how can every person born in the same 365 days have the same personality(?) – you're quite right. The birth year is only the beginning.

Your birth year reflects the way others see you and your basic characteristics, but your month and time of birth are also ruled by the celestial animals – probably different animals from the one that dominates your birth year. The personalities of these other animals modify and add talents to those you acquired with your birth year creature.

The 1920s

5 February 1924 – 24 January 1925 | RAT

25 January 1925 – 12 February 1926 | OX

13 February 1926 – 1 February 1927 | TIGER

CHAPTER 2: THE RABBIT

Rabbit Years

2 February 1927 – 22 January 1928

19 February 1939 – 7 February 1940

6 February 1951 – 26 January 1952

25 January 1963 – 12 February 1964

11 February 1975 – 30 January 1976

29 January 1987 – 16 February 1988

6 February 1999 – 4 February 2000

3 February 2011 – 22 January 2012

22 January 2023 – 9 February 2024

Natural Element: Wood

Will 2023 be a Golden Year for the Rabbit?

Congratulations Rabbit – you've just been given the keys to the kingdom. Well, the whole world, actually. 2023 is YOUR year! Your unique energy, your values, your special way of tackling things will be the right way for everyone in 2023 – whether they like it or not!

So, yes, this should certainly be a golden year for all bobtails. In fact, if you can't make 2023 phenomenal, you might as well give up the Rabbit struggle and try identifying as a different sign from now on.

Unlike some of your zodiac cousins, 2022 won't have been too disheartening for you if you're typical of your sign. Surprisingly, the Tiger and the Rabbit have an amicable relationship and can get along quite well together. Yet, despite this, many a Rabbit will have found themselves overwhelmed and exhausted at times during 2022 because Tiger energy is just so strong and demanding. There were probably times when everything seemed too fast, too loud, too much.

Well, happily, that's all over now. Now you get to dictate the pace – and the volume!

Suddenly, you're getting yourself noticed. Powerful people – the boss? – will go out of their way to help you. They want to say 'yes' to your elegant plans. Projects you began last year are particularly favoured – likely to leap into astonishing life with hardly any extra effort on your part.

In fact, this year, Rabbits are destined to stumble across a way to work smarter rather than harder – which will result in more leisure time without any loss of income. Stand by to watch the Rabbit coffers grow pleasingly as the year speeds on.

Yet, despite your good fortune, this is not the ideal time to change jobs. 2023 is more about building on what you've started, watching it flourish and taking delight in the success you've created.

According to Chinese tradition, being ruler of the year can bring its own difficulties. After all, being in charge brings responsibilities as well as privileges. The buck stops with the boss – and that's not always a pleasant prospect.

Yet, this year, the tradition could affect you differently, Rabbit. The sensitive Rabbit energy is likely to have soothed most irritations before they could trouble you. It's more likely many Rabbits will find themselves longing to return to their roots instead, or to discover their roots if they haven't already found them.

Places, faces, and family from the past will tug at your mind and draw you back, often literally. Many a Rabbit could decide to relocate to a childhood hometown or holiday destination where they spent many happy summers.

Old friends, old hobbies, old pastimes will suddenly demand to be enjoyed all over again, and you're likely to wonder why you ever let them slide for so long. It's not so much a step backwards as a recalibration. The chance to quietly enrich and expand your life by picking up some treasures that got lost along the way.

The gentler Water element of the year is also especially beneficial. This is because – like the Tiger – the Rabbit is believed to belong to the Wood family of creatures. Wood in Chinese astrology doesn't just represent trees and timber furniture, it's a symbol of the powerful force that causes grass to spring up from the ground and acorns to burst into the kind of growth that creates towering oaks.

And, of course, what wood needs most to help it flourish is a good supply of water.

With the Water element pushing you on this year, Rabbit, you can float happily along, letting the current sweep you to success in every area of your life.

This is the perfect time for baby bunnies to join the burrow, for family weddings or just any excuse to celebrate and have fun. Enjoy your special year, Rabbit!

What it Means to Be a Rabbit

We all love Rabbits, don't we? After the possibly dull Ox, and terrifying Tiger, the soft and pretty Rabbit seems like a welcome relief. We can all relate to the Rabbit. Big brown eyes, powder puff tail, cute little quivering nose, and an endearing way of hopping neatly around – nobody could take offence at the Rabbit.

In fact, nobody could feel threatened by the Rabbit in any way unless they happen to be a carrot, or a salad vegetable.

Yet, in the West, not all zodiac Rabbits are proud of their sign. They believe it suggests vulnerability and lack of drive. In the East, however, the Rabbit is appreciated for some very important qualities.

Like the Rat, Rabbits are brilliant survivors; they thrive and colonise in all manner of difficult terrains but, unlike the Rat, they manage to do this – mostly – without enraging or disgusting anyone, bar a few irritated farmers.

For all their cuddly looks, these are tough little creatures, frequently under-estimated. It's no accident that in the Chinese calendar, the defenceless, non-swimming Rabbit still manages to cross the river in fourth place, way ahead of stronger, abler creatures with seemingly much more going for them.

People born under this sign are never flashy or loud. Enter a crowded room, and the Rabbit wouldn't be the first person you notice. Yet, after a while, a stylish, immaculately-turned-out character would draw your eye. Classy and understated with perfect hair and graceful gestures – the typical Rabbit. This effortlessly polished aura is a gift. A Rabbit can emerge soaked to the skin from a rainstorm in a muddy field and within minutes appear clean, unruffled, and co-ordinated. Even Rabbits don't know how they do it. They're not even aware they *are* doing it.

Rabbits are refined with cultured tastes. They love beautiful things and art of all kinds, and hate to be surrounded by untidiness and disorder. Harmony is very important to the Rabbit – both visually and emotionally. People born in Rabbit years are sensitive in every way. They hate loud noises, loud voices, heavy traffic, and general ugliness. Quarrels can actually make them ill.

Yet this loathing of discord doesn't mean the Rabbit retires from the world. Rabbits somehow manage to end up near the centre of the action and tend to walk away with what they want, without appearing to have made any visible effort to get it.

Softly-spoken Rabbits are natural diplomats. Discreet and tactful, they can always find the right words; the perfect solutions to keep everybody happy. In fact, their powers of persuasion are so sophisticated that people usually do what Rabbit wants in the belief it's their own idea. This approach is so successful that Rabbit can't understand why other signs resort to argument and challenge, when so much more can be achieved through quiet conversation and compromise.

Rabbits tend to be brilliant strategists. When other egos get too distracted, jockeying for position and trying to be in charge for the task in hand, Rabbit deftly assesses the situation and has a plan worked out before the others have even agreed an agenda. Outwardly modest, Rabbits rarely admit to being ambitious, so they often end up being underestimated. Yet, privately, Rabbits can be single-minded and determined, even ruthless at times. These qualities, combined with their diplomatic skills and calm efficiency, seem to propel them smoothly to the top of whatever profession they've chosen.

Rabbits love their homes, which naturally are as beautiful and harmonious as they are. Home is a sanctuary and Rabbits take a lot of pleasure in choosing just the right pieces and décor to make their special place perfect, but in a comfortable way. Tidiness comes easily to them, and they can bring order to chaos quickly and neatly with the minimum of fuss. They enjoy entertaining – preferably small, informal gatherings of good friends – and they make wonderful hosts. Since they are such agreeable types, they're popular with everyone, and a Rabbit's invitation to dinner is accepted with eagerness.

When life is calm and secure, the Rabbit is perfectly happy to stay in one place. These types are not desperate for novelty though they do enjoy a relaxing holiday. Extreme sports are unlikely to appeal, but gentle exercise in beautiful surroundings soothes their nerves, and if they can take in an art gallery or a historic church followed by a delicious meal, they'd be truly contented bunnies.

Best Jobs for Rabbits 2023

Art Gallery Guide

Therapist

Diplomat

Financial Advisor

Interior Designer

Antiques Expert

Personal Shopper

Perfect Partners

Cupid's arrow can strike anywhere at any time, of course, but once the novelty of new romance wears off, some relationships are easier to maintain than others. Here's a guide to the Rabbit's compatibility with other signs.

Rabbit with Rabbit

These two gorgeous creatures look like they're made for each other. Their relationship will always be calm, peaceful, and unruffled, and it goes without saying that their home could grace a glossy magazine. Yet though they never argue, the willingness of both partners to compromise could end up with neither ever quite doing what they want. Ultimately, they may find the spark goes out.

Rabbit with Dragon

Dragon is such a larger than life character, Rabbit could feel overwhelmed at times. Also, the Dragon can be rather noisy and over-dramatic, which would get on Rabbit's nerves. Yet they each admire the other's good points. If they could live next door to each other instead of under the same roof, a long-term relationship might work.

Rabbit with Snake

This subtle pair could make a good combination. They both understand the value of working behind the scenes and neither has any desire to wear themselves out on endless adventures. They share a love of art, fine things, and quiet pleasures, and they both enjoy an orderly home. These two could settle down very happily together.

Rabbit with Horse

This could be tricky. It's fairly unlikely that Horse and Rabbit would ever end up on a date, but if they did, and there was a strong attraction, it could lead to a love/hate relationship. Rabbit's neat and tidy ways would enrage Horse, and Horse's unpredictable moods and over-the-top reactions would annoy Rabbit. Soon, Horse is likely to bolt for the hills or Rabbit retreat to its burrow.

Rabbit with Goat

Happy-go-lucky Goat is very appealing to Rabbit, particularly as deep-down Rabbit is a bit of a worrier. They're both sociable without needing to be the centre of attention and would be happy to people-watch for hours and then cheerfully compare notes afterwards. Goat is tolerant of Rabbit's need for some regular alone time to recharge too, so this couple could be a successful match.

Rabbit with Monkey

Mercurial Monkey doesn't really 'get' Rabbit. The Monkey can appreciate how well Rabbit operates and sees this approach gets good results, but it's all too picky and slow for Monkey. Rabbit, on the other hand, is amused by Monkey's quick wit and clever ways but deplores Monkey's slapdash, sometimes devious tactics. Very unlikely to work out.

Rabbit with Rooster

Another difficult match. However unfair it seems, Rooster comes over as loud, boastful, and uncouth to Rabbit, while Rabbit appears dull, staid, and insufficiently admiring of Rooster's fine feathers to appeal to Rooster. These two just can't see below the surface of the other, and it would be surprising if they ended up together. Only to be considered by the very determined.

Rabbit with Dog

Despite the fact that in the outside world Rabbit could easily end up as Dog's dinner, the astrological pair get on surprisingly well. Dog appreciates Rabbit's careful, efficient ways and soft voice, while Rabbit admires Dog's energy and good intentions. Dog's lack of interest in the finer points of interior design might try Rabbit's patience, but with a little work these two could reach an understanding.

Rabbit with Pig

Pig is not quite as interested in fine dining as Rabbit being as happy to scoff a burger as a Cordon Bleu creation, but their shared love of the good things in life makes these two happy companions. Once again, Pig's spending habits might irritate Rabbit, but not too much as Rabbit is quite willing to splurge on lovely things for the home. A relationship would work well.

Rabbit with Rat

Rat finds Rabbit intriguing. Here is an attractive, stylish creature that doesn't feel the need to be pushy or take centre stage yet somehow manages to be at the heart of things, while Rabbit is flattered and entertained by witty Rat's attention. These two respect each other but long-term, Rat could be too overpowering unless they both agree to give each other space.

Rabbit with Ox

Ox finds Rabbit rather cute and appealing. Whether male or female, there's something about Rabbit's inner fluffiness that brings out Ox's highly-developed protective instincts. Rabbit, meanwhile, loves the Ox's reassuring presence, and the sense of security Ox provides. These two could get on very well together as long as refined Rabbit can overlook Ox's occasional down-to-earth – Rabbit might say 'coarse' – observations.

Rabbit with Tiger

Surprisingly, the Rabbit is not intimidated by Tiger's dangerous aura and this attitude immediately appeals to Tiger who enjoys a challenge. Rabbit's calm presence and clever way with words keeps Tiger interested, while Rabbit finds Tiger's adventurous tales entertaining. With care, these two could get on well together for years.

Rabbit Love 2023 Style

It's your year, Rabbit, and you're ready to rock. You might look all elegant and fastidious, but then don't they say the quiet ones are the naughtiest! Single Rabbits are extremely successful when it comes to romance and beguiling potential partners. The brash, showy signs might attract a lot of attention but – at the end of the evening – it's often quiet Rabbit that leaves with the partner of their choice.

This year, single Rabbits are not so likely to find their soul mate – but only because they're so in demand they don't have time to devote exclusively to one partner. You're so hot you might as well enjoy it, Rabbit. There's always next year for settling down.

Attached Rabbits, on the other hand, may feel closer than ever to their beloved. In fact, many a Rabbit will be inspired to lavish attention on their partner, doing everything they can to help them, including advancing their loved one's career. That might not sound romantic, but you'll love what they've got in mind to thank you.

Secrets of Success in 2023

Rabbit years are all about happiness, relaxation, and success through natural growth rather than flogging yourself to the edge of collapse.

All of which suits you perfectly, Rabbit. Yet there is a danger you can have too much of a good thing. Being the sensitive type, stress exhausts you and anxiety makes you nervous and indecisive, which is obviously to be avoided. But on the other hand, an over-relaxed Rabbit becomes almost too indolent to move.

Strangle any *mañana* impulses the minute they arise. Laid-back is one thing, comatose quite another, Rabbit. Create some sensible targets and deadlines for yourself and stick to them. Success will flow to you more easily than usual this year, but if you surround yourself with inspiring people who motivate you, you'll be amazed at the heights you can reach.

The Rabbit Year at a Glance

January – You can feel the energy building. Bide your time, don't rush. Pace yourself for your big year.

February – Get ready to flex your muscles. Interested glances are coming your way. Someone powerful starts to see you in a new light.

March – You're feeling good. An exciting offer at work makes your day, and an admirer amazes you.

April – A new recruit at work tries to lay down the law. Time for your diplomatic skills, perhaps?

May – A home makeover or complete relocation appeals. Double-check all the details before committing yourself.

June – An attractive person enters your orbit but will their moods prove too much? Don't go too far, too fast.

July – A windfall brightens your day and you and your bestie know just the way to spend it.

August – An annoying person could slow you down. Tact is your middle name, so keep silent and work round them.

September – Work's got in a tangle. You can sort it, but it will take more time than you want to spare. Stick with it and try to smile. You'll get your reward.

October – The boss thinks you're wonderful. Something to do with last month? Either way, a bonus has your name on it.

November – A new romance or second honeymoon? Either way, expect much wining and dining.

December – It's party time and you're ready to rock. A big celebration round at yours will have them talking for months.

Lucky colours for 2023: Red, Blue, Purple

Lucky numbers for 2023: 3, 4, 6

CHAPTER 3: THE DRAGON

Dragon Years

23 January 1928 – 9 February 1929

8 February 1940 – 26 January 1941

27 January 1952 – 13 February 1953

13 February 1964 – 1 February 1965

31 January 1976 – 17 February 1977

17 February 1988 – 5 February 1989

5 February 2000 – 23 January 2001

23 January 2012 – 9 February 2013

10 February 2024 – 28 January 2025

Natural Element: Wood

Will 2023 be a Golden Year for the Dragon?

Wow. Dragon, the news just gets better and better. 2022 should have been an improvement on 2021 (how could it not, you're probably asking yourself), and now 2023 is set to be an improvement on 2022. A big improvement.

To be fair, if you're typical of your sign you should have come through the past year pretty well, but there have been undeniable ups and downs. You're never the type to avoid a drama, Dragon, so deep down you're probably not too bothered. The trouble is, you and the Tiger are a pretty feisty pair and when you disagree, the sparks certainly fly – which, since there's a Dragon involved, can lead to quite a conflagration.

Happily, for the homestead and your nearest and dearest, that's about to change in 2023. The gentle, peaceable Rabbit will not rile that fiery temper of yours, and though bunny pace is a little slower than you enjoy, the playful, buoyant vibes Rabbit generates, soothe your restless mind and appeal to your sense of fun. Remember fun, Dragon? In short supply for so long? Well, now it's back.

Wonderful career opportunities sprout around you like a newly sown lawn, this year, courtesy of the Rabbit, Dragon. This is because, though you and the Rabbit are not the most natural of friends – to be frank, Rabbit finds you a bit overwhelming – the two of you make excellent business partners.

Perhaps it's down to the version of the horoscope cycle story that involves Dragon saving Rabbit's life by softly blowing his log to safety on the riverbank.

Maybe ever afterwards Rabbit feels impelled to return the favour and help Dragon wherever possible.

But whatever the reason, this year, the cash and the success will flow without so much hard work. Where the Tiger demanded you earn every scrap of good fortune and demonstrate your worthiness for big cat favours, the Rabbit smiles on each sincere effort and hands over the goodies without a struggle.

Yet this is not the year to be fixated on that famous Dragon hoard. In fact, there's a chance some foolish hastiness could lead to a financial loss. But don't be downhearted, Dragon. This is Rabbit's way of getting you to concentrate on other important aspects in your life – things that are more important than treasure – and in any case, you'll soon earn back whatever you've lost, and more, before the year's end.

Something you were working on last year that was developing well could blossom in a most surprising and unexpected way. In fact, fame and fortune could be beckoning for many a Dragon. Yet the most delightful part of this success story is that it falls into place so easily. The sense of pressure and deadlines to be met has melted away, and despite your workaholic tendencies, you find you like it.

Good news concerning the family will please you in 2023, and it looks as if you'll be tempted away on more than one enjoyable holiday. In fact, you like where you find yourself so much, you could end up buying some sort of holiday home. Whether it's a caravan, a cabin, or a villa overlooking the sea, once you've discovered your little paradise, you'll return many times.

One thing to bear in mind is that next year, 2024, is *your* year – it's the Green (Wood) Dragon Year – the beginning of a whole new Dragon cycle. So, for you, 2023 is a bit like a New Year's Eve that lasts all year. You're looking back as well as forward; finishing off and refining any outstanding issues from the past 12 years, assessing lessons learned, ready to leap forward on a whole new adventure in 2024.

Which is another reason why 2023 is a great excuse for you to party.

What it Means to Be a Dragon

To be honest, Dragon, it's not really fair. Your sign has so many advantages. When you're on good form, your personality is so dazzling the other signs need sunglasses.

The only mythical creature in the celestial cycle, in China the Dragon is associated with the Emperor and revered as a symbol of protection, power, and magnificence. No New Year celebration would be complete without the colourful Dragon, dancing through the streets, twisting and turning, and banishing evil spirits.

The Dragon is regarded as the most fortunate of signs and every couple hopes for a Dragon baby. A child born in a Dragon year is believed to bring good luck to the whole family and, to this day, the birth rate tends to rise about 5% in the Chinese community in Dragon years.

Dragons are usually strong, healthy, and blessed with enormous self-confidence and optimism. Even if they're not conventionally good-looking, they stand out in a crowd. They're charismatic with magnetic personalities, formidable energy, and people look up to them. Dragons are so accustomed to attention, they rarely question why this should be the case. It just seems like the natural way of the world.

These people think BIG. They're visionaries, bubbling with original new ideas, and their enthusiasm is so infectious, their optimism so strong, they easily inspire others. Without even trying, Dragons are born leaders and happily sweep their teams of followers into whatever new venture they've just dreamed up.

The only downside to this is that Dragons are easily bored. Trivial matters – such as details – irritate them, and they're keen to rush on to the next challenge before they've quite finished the first.

With a good second in command, who can attend to the picky minutiae, all could be well. If not, Dragon's schemes can go spectacularly wrong. Yet it hardly seems to matter. The Dragon ascribes to the theory that you have to fail your way to success. Setbacks are quickly forgotten as Dragon launches excitedly into the next adventure and quite often – given the Dragon's good luck – this works.

People born under this sign often receive success and wealth, yet they are not materialistic. They're generous and kind in an absent-minded way, and care far more about having a worthy goal than any rewards it might bring. And it is vital for the Dragon to have a goal. A Dragon without a goal is a sad, dispirited creature – restless and grumpy.

Even if it's not large, the Dragon home gives the impression of space and light. Dragons hate to feel confined in any way. They like to look out the window and see lots of sky and have clear, uncluttered surfaces around them, even if it's difficult for Dragons to keep them that way.

Yet the Dragon home could have a curiously un-lived-in feel. This is because the Dragon regards home as a lair – a comfortable base from which to plan the next project, rather than a place to spend a lot of time.

Dragons love to travel, but they don't really mind where they go as long as it's different and interesting. Yet, despite so much going for them, Dragons often feel misunderstood. Their impatience with trivia extends to the irritating need for tact and diplomacy at times. Dragon doesn't get this. If Dragon has something to say, they say it. Why waste time dressing it up in fancy words they think? But then people get upset, and Dragon is baffled. It's not always easy being a Dragon.

Best Jobs for Dragon 2023

Member of a Royal Family(!)

Movie Star

Journalist

Barrister

Scientist

TV Producer

Architect

Headteacher

Perfect Partners

Cupid's arrow can strike anywhere at any time, of course, but once the novelty of new romance wears off, some relationships are easier to maintain than others. Here's a guide to the Dragon's compatibility with other signs.

Dragon with Dragon

When Dragon meets Dragon, onlookers tend to take a step back and hold their breath. These two are a combustible mix – they either love each other or loathe each other. They are so alike it could go either way. Both dazzling in their own orbits, they can't fail to notice the other's charms, but since they both need to be centre stage, things could get competitive. With give and take and understanding this match could work well, but it won't be easy.

Dragon with Snake

Surprisingly, this couple gets along beautifully. Snake's elegant appearance and quick but subtle mind intrigues Dragon, while Snake admires Dragon's success and endless energy. Snake has no need to battle for the limelight and is quite happy to sit back and support Dragon's schemes from the comfort of a stylish sofa. Which is all the encouragement Dragon needs.

Dragon with Horse

The athletic Horse is pretty good at keeping up with dashing Dragon. And Dragon appreciates a partner who enjoys getting out and about as much as Dragon does. Yet Horse might grow weary of Dragon's constant new projects and resent having to be involved. Horse likes to go off and do Horsey things at frequent intervals which Dragon tends to view as disloyal. This relationship could get fiery.

Dragon with Goat

Goat tends to baffle the busy Dragon. Dragon can see Goat is the creative type but can't understand why Goat doesn't appear to be working very hard when so much could be achieved. In fact, if they stayed together long enough, Dragon could help Goat make the most of many talents, but it's unlikely either of them can sustain enough interest for this to happen.

Dragon with Monkey

These two are likely to hit it off immediately. Each is attracted to the other's intelligence and lively presence, and Dragon's exuberance doesn't overwhelm hyperactive Monkey. What's more, though they both enjoy being surrounded by a crowd, Monkey only wants to make people laugh while Dragon hopes to inspire them to a cause. There is no conflict, so this couple can help each other to go far.

Dragon with Rooster

A Dragon and Rooster pairing will always attract attention. These two are both gorgeous beings and love to be surrounded by admirers. They will probably enjoy going out together and being seen as a couple, but in the long-term, they may not be able to provide the kind of support each secretly needs.

Entertaining for a while but probably not a lasting relationship.

Dragon with Dog

Not the easiest of combinations. Down-to-earth Dog can't see what all the fuss is about when it comes to Dragons. Unimpressed by glamour and irritated by what seems to Dog the gullibility of Dragon admirers, Dog can't be bothered to find out more. Dragon meanwhile is hurt by Dog's lack of interest. Great determination would be needed to make this work.

Dragon with Pig

While Dragon and Pig might seem to be opposites, the two of them can create a surprisingly contented relationship. Pig is quite happy for Dragon to fly around doing exciting things as long as Pig is not expected to do much more than admire profusely. Dragon appreciates Pig's uncritical support and makes allowances for Pig's lack of stamina. This couple could live in harmony.

Dragon with Rat

This couple is usually regarded as a very good match. They have much in common being action-loving, excitement-seeking personalities who hate to be bored. It takes a lot to dazzle Rat, but the Dragon's glamorous aura proves irresistible, while Dragon loves to be admired, so each enjoys being with the other. There could be the odd power struggle as these two are both strong characters but the magnetism is so intense they usually kiss and make up.

Dragon with Ox

Chalk and cheese though this pair may appear to be, there's a certain fascination between them. Ox may not approve of Dragon's showy manner but recognises Dragon's good intentions, while Dragon admires Ox's strength of character and gift for completing tasks. If each could find a way to tolerate the other's wildly different lifestyles, they might be good for each other but, long-term, Dragon's hectic pace might wear down even the Ox's legendary stamina.

Dragon with Tiger

The two biggest personalities in the zodiac would seem bound to clash. After all, these larger than life characters share so many similarities there's a danger they'd compete. Yet a relationship between the Tiger and Dragon often works well. They understand each other's impulsive natures, but they're also different enough to supply the support the other needs. They'd make a formidable power couple.

Dragon with Rabbit

Dragon is such a larger than life character, Rabbit could feel overwhelmed at times. Also, the Dragon can be rather noisy and over-dramatic, which would get on Rabbit's nerves. Yet they each admire the other's good points. If they could live next door to each other instead of under the same roof, a long-term relationship might work.

Dragon Love 2023 Style

So, are you ready for a break, Dragon? Last year, once you got away from work, all you wanted to do was party. Hopefully, you're all danced out now because it looks like 2023 is more about love.

Single Dragons will attract their effortless attention as usual, but this year they'll be returning the flirty glances coming their way. Someone special could well catch your eye, and this time you won't be in a hurry to spread those fabulous wings and zoom away. Exclusive just got more interesting, Dragon. Maybe the two of you could explore the concept more deeply.

Attached Dragons find themselves in second honeymoon mood even if they never got around to getting married in the first place. Maybe this year you'll decide on that splendid wedding you promised yourself someday – and if you've already got the tee shirt, maybe you'll feel sentimental enough to renew your vows.

Secrets of Success in 2023

It's all so much easier this year, Dragon, you could be forgiven for thinking you need only sit back and polish your claws while Rabbit wafts treasure into your lap without you stirring a wing tip.

But, of course, it's not that simple. The Rabbit makes demands, even if they're expressed so quietly you scarcely notice them. And Rabbit expects these demands to be met.

So, this year, Dragons are being asked to compromise, to work harmoniously with others, and to listen to other people's points of view.

As your confidence increases, Dragon, there's a danger you'll get so carried away with your latest brilliant idea, you'll dash off – all fired with enthusiasm – completely failing to take other people's opinions into account.

Yet this approach could prove disastrous. For a start, your colleagues could have something valuable to contribute, which you'll miss, but worse, ignoring them could lead to resentment, which will work against you. Right now, you need to pay great attention to the people in your orbit. Particularly any new faces. Some of them may not be what they seem, and a false friend could harm your prospects.

So just ease up a bit, Dragon; listen as much as you speak – more if possible – and borrow a little Rabbit diplomacy. You'll be amazed at the difference.

The Dragon Year at a Glance

January – There's a zing in the air, a tingle in your toes, and you can hardly wait for the new opportunities you can sense on the breeze.

February – An intriguing offer comes your way from an unexpected quarter. Consider it carefully.

March – The Dragon pad is looking a little exhausted. Time for some of that 100mph TLC for which you're famous. Try not to be too slapdash.

April – An exciting project is reaching fruition. The outlook is excellent. Champagne on ice?

May – Cash is rolling in, and friends want to help you celebrate. Why argue? Just don't be too extravagant.

June – You keep getting presented with holiday ideas. Don't resist. Explore widely. You may discover your special place.

July – A face from the past gets in touch. It's good to see them, but is there an ulterior motive?

August – Eccentric vibes are developing, Dragon, and you're intrigued to see where an unusual plan may lead. Follow your instincts.

September – Surprising news from a colleague or friend. They could use your help. Don't hold back.

October – Someone irritating crosses your path. A neighbour, traffic warden, or colleague. Totally unreasonable, but don't incinerate them. Think Rabbit.

November – Are you about to become famous? Everyone wants to know you all of a sudden.

December – Party time has come round again, and you've got a lot to celebrate. Share the good fortune around.

Lucky colours for 2023: Red, Silver, Gold

Lucky numbers for 2023: 1, 5, 2

CHAPTER 4: THE SNAKE

Snake Years

10 February 1929 – 29 January 1930

27 January 1941 – 14 February 1942

14 February 1953 – 2 February 1954

2 February 1965 – 20 January 1966

18 February 1977 – 6 February 1978

6 February 1989 – 26 January 1990

24 January 2001 – 11 February 2002

10 February 2013 – 30 January 2014

29 January 2025 – 16 February 2026

Natural Element: Fire

Will 2023 be a Golden Year for the Snake?

So, is that a great big smile on your face, Snake? If it's not, it soon will be. 2023 is set to be just the kind of year you enjoy best.

Last year, despite your dignified protests, the Tiger forced you to exert yourself in ways that probably made you feel uncomfortable at times.

You resent being rushed and loathe being obliged to tackle issues before you're ready, but under Tiger's rule there wasn't much choice.

The trouble was, you and Tiger have never been on the same wavelength. Never were, never will be. Ideally, if you could choose your own boss, Tiger would be more or less bottom of the list, so a year when Tiger's in charge was always going to need delicate handling.

Fortunately, 2023 is quite different. Snake and Rabbit are good friends. The Rabbit understands your constitution and your need to pace yourself. The calmer atmosphere and lower stress levels Rabbit energy generates help you relax and concentrate on the important things in life.

Last year, the frantic Tiger probably had you pouring far more time than you wanted into financial affairs, career matters, and even complicated legal situations. These may not even have been your own issues – you may have been dragged into assisting someone else. But whatever the cause, it meant that other matters essential to the Snake's wellbeing tended to get pushed aside.

Family, friends, and your all-important home went to the back of the queue. Some people felt distinctly neglected.

Well, this year, you can restore the balance. One of the great things about the Snake/Rabbit relationship is that the Snake belongs to the Fire family of animals, while the Rabbit is from the Wood family.

Although Wood can be a little nervous around Fire in some situations, it's also true that Wood feeds Fire. So with a friendly Wood creature running the year, the Snake will never go hungry.

This means that in 2023, instead of worrying about career matters, you can let work take care of itself and concentrate on rebuilding your links with family and friends. New arrivals may be about to brighten the scene, and you could either be moving to a new home or organising an exciting revamp to the current Snake quarters.

Big family gatherings are ringed in red on the Snake calendar, too, alongside many shared holidays which will be remembered for years to come.

Some slight disappointments could occur due to the Water element of the year. Water, of course, doesn't suit Snake's Fire too well, though it's less of a problem in 2023 under the Rabbit's modifying influence.

Water helps cash and opportunities flow, but on encountering Snake's Fiery flames, they tend to fizzle out. This suggests that some projects or deals that initially looked promising could suddenly evaporate like steam from a kettle, leaving many a baffled Snake wondering what went wrong.

Yet, chances are, other aspects of the Serpent life more than make up for a few disappointments. Spiritually-inclined Snakes will make fascinating discoveries this year. Some may even create some sort of sanctuary which draws visitors from afar. Others may develop a previously unsuspected artistic talent. 2023 will be the year you learn far more about *yourself* than you ever suspected, Snake, and it will set the tone of your life for years to come.

What it Means to Be a Snake

Imagine, for a moment, a creature that was incredibly beautiful, wise, intelligent, graceful, sophisticated and respected. A creature always unhurried, yet attaining its goals, apparently without effort.

What would you call this amazing beast? Well if you were Chinese, you'd probably call it a Snake. That's right – a Snake.

Here, in the West, Snakes are almost as unwelcome as Rats and have been ever since Eve was persuaded to eat that apple in the Garden of Eden by a wily serpent. Most of us wouldn't have a good word to say for Snakes. Yet, in the East, it's a different story. There, all manner of positive qualities are discerned in the Snake, and the zodiac Snake is a good sign to be born under.

What's more, if we can forget all preconceived notions and look afresh at the much-maligned serpent, we have to admit there's something quite remarkable – almost magical – about the Snake.

For a start, Snakes don't have eyelids, which makes their stare particularly disconcerting. Astonishingly, they can shed their entire skins without ill effect, and slide away with a brand new, rejuvenated, wrinkle-free body – a feat many a human would envy.

Then there's the way they slither along without the need for legs – a bit repellent to a lot of people, but it can't be denied there's something uncanny about it. It's a surprisingly efficient means of locomotion too, and at times Snakes can move with astonishing speed. Quite a few of them can do this in water as well as on land, which makes them remarkably adaptable.

Snakes are in no way cuddly, but it seems even in the West we've retained a faint memory of a time when we recognised wisdom in the serpent. The Rod of Asclepius – the familiar symbol of a snake twisted around a pole – is still a widely used and recognised medical sign, seen outside pharmacies and doctors' surgeries, even if we don't know that Asclepius was the Greek God associated with healing. And in Greece, in the dim and distant past, snakes were sacred and believed to aid the sick.

The Chinese zodiac Snake is regarded as possibly the most beautiful of all the creatures, and people born under this sign somehow manage to present themselves in such an artful way, they give the illusion of beauty, even if not naturally endowed.

The Snake is physically graceful too. Each movement flowing into the next with effortless, elegant economy. Even when they're in a hurry, Snakes appear calm and unrushed, and should they arrive late for an appointment they're so charming and plausible with their excuses they're always forgiven.

This is a sign of great intelligence and subtlety. Snakes are never pushy, yet can usually slide into the heart of any situation they choose. Their clever conversation and easy charm makes them popular at any gathering. Yet, the Snake is picky. Snakes prefer to conserve their energy and don't waste it on activities and people of no interest to them. They are self-contained, quite happy with their own company if necessary, and seldom bored.

At work, Snakes are quietly ambitious, but in line with their policy of conserving energy wherever possible, they will aim for the quickest, easiest route to their goals. Just as the mythical Snake crossed the celestial river wrapped around the hoof of the Horse, the Snake is quite content to link their fortunes to those of a rising star so that Snake is carried to the top in their wake. Ever practical, the Snake has no need for an ego massage – the end result is what matters.

Other signs often mistake Snake's economy of action for laziness, but this is short-sighted. In fact, the Snake is so efficient and so clever that tasks are completed with great speed, leaving Snake with plenty of time to relax afterwards. What's more, in the same way that a Snake can shed its skin, people born under this sign are quite capable of suddenly walking out of a situation or way of life that no longer suits them, and reinventing themselves elsewhere without regret.

They tend to do this without warning, leaving their previous companions stunned. Only afterwards do people learn that the Snake has been inert and silently brooding for months. But it's no good imploring Snake to return. Snake's actions are swift and irrevocable.

The Snake home is a lovely place. Snakes have perfect taste. They like art, design, good lighting, and comfort. They're excellent hosts. They may not often entertain, unless they can delegate the chores, but when they do, they make it a stylish occasion to remember.

Snakes are known for their love of basking in the sun, and zodiac Snakes are no exception. Trips involving long hikes uphill in the pouring rain will not impress the Snake, but a smart sun-lounger by an infinity pool in a tropical paradise… well, that would be Snake's idea of heaven.

Best Jobs for Snake

Counsellor

Fashion Boutique Manager

Interior Designer

Aromatherapist

Hairdresser

Tarot Card Reader

Political Advisor

Perfect Partners

Cupid's arrow can strike anywhere at any time, of course, but once the novelty of new romance wears off, some relationships are easier to maintain than others. Here's a guide to the Snake's compatibility with other signs.

Snake with Snake

This fine looking couple turn heads wherever they go. Beautiful and perfectly dressed these two look like the perfect match. They never stop talking and enjoy the same interests so this could be a successful relationship. Long-term, however, there could be friction. They're both experts at getting what they want using the same sophisticated techniques, so they can see through each other.

Snake with Horse

At some level, perhaps, Horse remembers how Snake beat him in the calendar race, so despite an initial attraction, these two could be wary of each other. Snake is impressed by Horse's energy and athleticism while Horse admires Snake's elegance and charm. Yet they don't really have much in common. Deep thinking Snake could find Horse rather shallow and Horse may see Snake as frustratingly enigmatic.

Snake with Goat

Snake and Goat could enjoy many happy hours touring art galleries and exhibitions together. Neither of them craves excitement and harsh, adrenaline-boosting activities, and both appreciate creative artistic personalities. There's no pressure to compete with each other so these two would sail along quite contentedly. Not a passionate alliance but they could be happy.

Snake with Monkey

These two clever creatures ought to admire each other if only for their fine minds and, at first, it's possible they might. But unless they're really determined to make it work, it won't be long before active Monkey finds

Snake's energy-saving ways irritating, while Snake loses patience with Monkey's endless jokes.

Snake with Rooster

Surprisingly, Snake and Rooster work well together. Both gorgeous in different ways, they complement each other without competing. Snake's keen eyes can see beneath Rooster's proud facade to the sensitive, unsure person inside, while Rooster appreciates Snake's unobtrusive strength and wise words of encouragement at just the right moment. These two could be inseparable.

Snake with Dog

Some snakes seem to have an almost hypnotic power and, for some reason, Dog is particularly susceptible to these skills. We've heard of snake-charmers, but snakes can be dog-charmers and, without even trying, Snakes can find themselves the recipients of Dog devotion. Since the Dog is strong, loyal, and can be fun, Snake is not averse to this but might, in the end, find it boring.

Snake with Pig

Pig and Snake don't have a lot to say to each other. Snake can't be bothered with Pig's endless shopping, and Pig is hurt by Snake's snobbish attitude. They both enjoy the good things in life so a luxury fling could briefly be fun – a shared spa break might be a good idea – but in the long-term, this relationship is probably not worth pursuing.

Snake with Rat

The Snake shares Rat's good taste and being elegant, sophisticated, and smart will delight Rat at first sight. These two get on very well on an intellectual level but perhaps are better as good friends rather than long-term partners. The Snake's love of basking in the sun for hours strikes Rat as lazy and dull, while Rat's need to rush around doing deals and meeting people seems pointless and wearying to Snake.

Snake with Ox

Like Ox, the Snake is quietly ambitious and not given to racing around unless it's absolutely necessary. Ox, on the other hand, respects Snake's clever brain and understated elegance. These two could quickly discover how beneficial an alliance between them would be. They're both happy to give the other space when required but also step in with support when needed. This could be a very successful match.

Snake with Tiger

Not the best of romances. These two are so fundamentally different that any initial attraction is unlikely to last. Snake likes to bask and soak up the sun while Tiger wants to explore and discover. Tiger takes in the big picture at a glance and is off to the next challenge while Snake likes to pause, delve beneath the surface, and consider matters. It wouldn't take long before these two annoy each other.

Snake with Rabbit

This subtle pair could make a good combination. They both understand the value of working behind the scenes and neither has any desire to wear themselves out on endless adventures. They share a love of art, fine things, and quiet pleasures and they both enjoy an orderly home. These two could settle down very happily together.

Snake with Dragon

Surprisingly, this couple gets along beautifully. Snake's elegant appearance and quick but subtle mind intrigues Dragon, while Snake admires Dragon's success and endless energy. Snake has no need to battle for the limelight and is quite happy to sit back and support Dragon's schemes from the comfort of a stylish sofa. Zoom

Which is all the encouragement Dragon needs.

Snake Love 2023 Style

The irritating thing about Snakes, as far as love-rival signs are concerned, is that the single Snake appears to be completely unmoved by any array of prospective partners on offer. At parties, they lounge, elegantly aloof in the corner of the room, apparently more interested in their drink and their thoughts than introducing themselves to an admirer. Yet, somehow, at the end of the evening, they manage to waltz off with the fittest singleton in the room without a backward glance.

Could it be some form of hypnosis the rivals wonder in despair? Well, whatever the secret, single Snakes are at it again this year. You are irresistible, Snake, and you know it. Enjoy.

Attached Snakes are more than usually inclined to spoil their partners in 2023 after being too preoccupied to bother much last year. This probably comes as a welcome surprise to the partner, since it's often the other way round, but as long as they're suitably grateful, domestic bliss reigns.

Secrets of Success in 2023

Snake standards are very high, so the first thing you have to consider, Snake, is how you *choose* to define success.

You've got everything going for you this year, but your best successes will be emotional – finding joy with loved ones, widening your circle of friends, and helping others whenever you get the chance.

The only way to slip up is by becoming so relaxed under the tranquil influence of the Rabbit that you either can't be bothered to leave the comfort of your newly splendid home, or alternatively you forget yourself and allow your critical tongue to say out loud what you were thinking inside.

Because, let's face it, Snake, you have laser vision when it comes to noticing when anyone else makes a mistake, chooses unflattering clothes, or generally fails to perform as effortlessly as you do. You can't help being so clever, of course, but it's not a good idea to keep reminding people. Why make enemies unnecessarily? So smile sweetly, keep your opinions to yourself, and you'll have a wonderful year.

Snake Year at a Glance

January – The Tiger year is coming to an end, and you'll not be sorry to see it go. Hectic times are not really your thing. Prepare to drop that burden.

February – The pressure is easing, but there are still some issues from last year to hold you up. Grit your teeth and work through them methodically.

March – Spring makes you smile. New romance is stirring. Should you take up their offer?

April – A demanding authority figure is taking up your time. They are impressed with you, so don't be rebellious.

May – Happy news inspires the family circle. A new baby, a new home, or even a new pet delights everyone.

June – One of your sporty mates is trying to tempt you into the great outdoors. Fresh air may do you good.

July – Mystic vibes swirl around this month. Are you unexpectedly psychic, or is it just a series of coincidences?

August – Holiday season comes round again, but you'll prefer several short breaks. Why restrict yourself to just one place?

September – Flashy types don't usually appeal, but a boisterous newcomer arouses your interest. Give them a chance.

October – Duty calls. Someone who looks up to you requires your aid, and you can't really say no. Earn some good Karma.

November – Christmas shopping is more fun than usual this year and it's one of your talents. Enjoy, but don't max out your credit card.

December – It looks like you'll be going away for the festivities. Pack a big suitcase!

Lucky colours for 2023: Black, Purple, Emerald

Lucky numbers for 2023: 3, 7, 8

CHAPTER 5: THE HORSE

Horse Years

30 January 1930 – 16 February 1931

15 February 1942 – 4 February 1943

3 February 1954 – 23 January 1955

21 January 1966 – 8 February 1967

7 February 1978 – 27 January 1979

27 January 1990 – 14 February 1991

12 February 2002 – 31 January 2003

31 January 2014 – 18 February 2015

17 February 2026 – 5 February 2027

Natural Element: Fire

Will 2023 be a Golden Year for the Horse?

You're on a roll, Horse. Last year you were one of the lucky signs, and guess what, it looks like you're a winner again in 2023! What are the chances?

Okay, so maybe in 2022, you didn't actually win the lottery, become a household name, or end up as the first Horse in space. But, nevertheless, if you're typical of your sign, you did pretty well. More went right than wrong.

Your good fortune was down to the fact that the Tiger of 2022 just loves his buddy, the Horse. You had encouragement and support behind the scenes throughout the year, and if you were a sensible, Horse, you made the most of it.

The terrific news is that though the Rabbit is not quite as enamoured of you as the Tiger – you can be a bit too wild and unpredictable at times to appeal wholeheartedly to Rabbit sensibilities – tolerant Rabbit is quite prepared to support you and your projects from a safe distance.

What's more, the aspects that made 2022 so fortunate for most Horses are revisiting in 2023 – albeit in slightly modified form – so you can benefit from them all over again.

Last year was ideal for many Horses to start their own businesses, gain new professional qualifications, put in for promotion, or strike out in any number of exciting new directions. This year, Rabbit energy will help you develop all these ventures and whip them on to even greater success.

If you didn't quite get around to making a start on your big dreams last year, Horse, there's still time under the generous influence of the Rabbit, but don't delay. These favourable conditions might not be on offer next year.

Like the Tiger of 2022, the Rabbit is regarded as belonging to the Wood family of creatures, while the Horse is from the Fire tribe.

This means that since Wood is very beneficial for Fire, constantly feeding it and making it stronger, Fire creatures can flourish when a Wood animal is in charge. True, this can make for a slightly uneasy relationship as hungry Fire can exhaust Wood with its constant demands – so the secret, Horse, is to be as self-reliant as possible. Curb those reckless impulses, so you don't need to call on your loyal Wood friends to come to your rescue so often. This is particularly important in 2023 because Rabbit energy isn't as strong as Tiger energy. You don't want to use up a whole year's luck by August.

No year is completely perfect, of course, and any glitches are likely to be caused by the Water element that imbues 2023 just as it did 2022. Under the gentle Rabbit, this energy lacks the force it had when associated with the Tiger, but even so, a wash of water can have an annoyingly dampening effect on Horse's Fiery fortunes.

The good thing about the Water element, of course, is that it's excellent for growing bank balances, and easing communication and creativity in every form. Cash will flow in your direction, Horse, and your wealth should be piling up in a most satisfactory way.

This year, though, you could find some projects or plans fizzling out for emotional reasons – another water-influenced area. Unexpected responsibilities involving family or close friends could suddenly demand your attention, and you may have to put some cherished ideas on pause for a while.

You could also encounter some unusually moody or completely illogical people who will quite unreasonably try to block your path. Don't paw the ground or bolt off in a huff, Horse; make like the Rabbit. Patiently explain (yet again) why your intentions are sound. Do not raise your voice, and if all else fails, find another route and work your way round them.

There's nothing the Horse likes more than a gathering of the clans – the bigger, the better – and 2023 promises some spectacular get-togethers. What's more, the relaxed atmosphere generated by the Rabbit is likely to lead to far less pressure at work and far more time and energy for travel. If you're typical of your sign, Horse, you just love to be on the move, preferably out of doors in a green setting, but you're not too picky as long as you can get going, and this year there'll be more trips than ever. Enjoy.

What it Means to Be a Horse

Sleek and graceful, as well as strong and swift, the Horse has always been an object of admiration and often longing. Young girls dream of having their own pony while many adults, on acquiring a pile of cash, often treat themselves to a racehorse or at least a share in one.

In China, the Horse is believed to be a symbol of freedom, and you've only got to see a picture of the famous white horses of the Camargue, exuberantly splashing through the marshes, to understand why.

People born in the year of the Horse exude a similar magnificence. They tend to be strong and athletic with broad shoulders and fine heads of thick hair. Where would the Horse be without its mane? Most Horses excel at sports, especially when young. They can run fast if they choose, but they will happily try any game until they find the one that suits them best.

Horses, being herd animals, are gregarious types and don't like to spend too long alone. They enjoying hanging out with a crowd, chatting and swapping gossip, and Horses of both sexes can lap up any amount of grooming. They love having their hair brushed and fussed over, their nails manicured; a facial or relaxing massage is usually welcome.

Yet, Horses are more complex than they first appear. The affable, easy-going charmer, delighting everyone at a party, can suddenly take offence at a casual remark or storm off in a huff over some tiny hitch almost unnoticeable to anyone else, leaving companions baffled. They tend to stay baffled too, because it's difficult to get a handle on what upsets the Horse since what annoys them one week may leave them completely unruffled the next.

The trouble is, although they look tough, Horses are, in fact, very sensitive. Inside, they're still half-wild. Their senses are incredibly sharp, and although they don't realise it, deep down they're constantly scanning the horizon and sniffing the air for the first signs of danger. As a result, Horses live on their nerves. They tend to over-react when things don't go completely to plan, and have to work hard to control a sense of panic. Ideally, Horses would like to bolt away when the going gets rough but as this is not usually possible, they get moody and difficult instead.

Provide calm, congenial conditions for a Horse, however, and you couldn't wish for a friendlier companion. The Horse is lively, enthusiastic, versatile, and fun.

At work, the Horse wants to do well but can't stand being fenced in or forced to perform repetitive, routine tasks. Also, although they're good in a team, Horses have a need for privacy and independence so they may change jobs frequently until they find the right role. Yet, when they're happy, Horses will shine.

At home, Horse is probably planning the next trip. Horses like to be comfortable but they're not the most domesticated of the signs. They love being in the open air and don't see the point of spending too much time wallowing on a sofa or polishing dusty ornaments. They may well spend more time in the garden than indoors. On holiday, Horse loves to head for wide-open spaces – a vast beach, a craggy hillside or a mountain meadow; Horse would be thrilled to explore them all.

Best Jobs for Horse

Jockey

Athlete

Ballet Teacher

Garden Designer

Swimming Coach

Kennel Manager

Perfect Partners

Cupid's arrow can strike anywhere at any time, of course, but once the novelty of new romance wears off, some relationships are easier to maintain than others. Here's a guide to the Horse's compatibility with other signs.

Horse with Horse

No doubt about it, these two make a magnificent couple, and any foals in the family would be spectacular. They certainly understand each other, particularly their shared need for both company and alone time so, in general, they get on well. The only tricky part could come if they both grew anxious over the same issue at the same time. Neither would find it easy to calm the other.

Horse with Goat

Goat and Horse just click! These two love kicking up their heels and trotting off into the green. Goat doesn't need to go far or do anything strenuous but is always up for a break in routine, while Horse doesn't do routine at all so is constantly on the lookout for a partner ready to escape. This couple rarely considers the consequences but, mostly, they don't need to.

Horse with Monkey

Uh oh – best not attempted unless it's love at first sight. Monkey and Horse have wildly different outlooks and can't seem to see eye to eye on anything. They're both lively but in different ways that don't complement each other. Monkey will consider Horse's moods illogical and pointless while Horse is irritated that Monkey makes no attempt to understand how Horse feels. Very hard work.

Horse with Rooster

The eye-catching Rooster intrigues Horse while Rooster appreciates Horse's strength and agility. They can enjoy many stimulating dates together. Yet, in the long-run, this couple may not be able to provide the stability the other needs. They're both sensitive types but in different ways. After a while, the relationship could run out of steam.

Horse with Dog

Both good friends of man, these two can make a formidable team. Dog understands the occasional need for solitude while admiring Horse's strength and agility. Horse, meanwhile, senses Dog's loyalty and down to earth nature. Both lovers of the great outdoors and physical activity, they'll never be short of adventures to share. A promising long-term relationship.

Horse with Pig

Pig and Horse are good companions. Horse is soothed by easy-going Pig and Pig is proud to be seen with such an alluring creature as Horse. They don't have a lot of interests in common, but they don't antagonise each other either. They can jog along amicably for quite a while, but long-term they may find they each want more than the other can provide.

Horse with Rat

Rat and Horse both fizz with energy, and they love action and looking good, yet this is not seen as an ideal partnership. Nothing's impossible of course, but these two will have to work hard to find harmony. The Rat will admire Horse's enthusiasm and cheerful approach but become impatient to discover Horse can also be fiery and emotional. Horse, on the other hand, can find Rat's risk-taking behaviour extremely worrying.

Horse with Ox

Long ago on many Western farms, Ox was replaced by the Horse, and it may be that Ox has never forgotten and never forgiven. At any rate, these two, despite both being big, strong animals are not usually friends. Horse is too flighty and frivolous to interest Ox for long, while Ox's methodical, careful ways will irritate the Horse. Best not to go there.

Horse with Tiger

This athletic pair gets on pretty well. They both like physical pursuits, testing their strength out of doors or just enjoying the feel of the wind in their hair and the ground under their feet. True, Horse may not quite understand Tiger's plans for world domination, but it doesn't really matter. Horse is happy to be loyal to such a charismatic partner. As they're both moody, there could be rows but making up is exciting.

Horse with Rabbit

This could be tricky. It's fairly unlikely that Horse and Rabbit would ever end up on a date, but if they did and there was a strong attraction, it could lead to a love/hate relationship. Rabbit's neat and tidy ways would enrage Horse and Horse's unpredictable moods and over-the-top reactions would annoy Rabbit. Soon, Horse is likely to bolt for the hills or Rabbit retreat to its burrow.

Horse with Dragon

The athletic Horse is pretty good at keeping up with dashing Dragon. And Dragon appreciates a partner who enjoys getting out and about as much as Dragon does. Yet Horse might grow weary of Dragon's constant new projects and resent having to be involved. Horse likes to go off and do Horsey things at frequent intervals which Dragon tends to view as disloyal. This relationship could get fiery.

Horse with Snake

At some level, perhaps Horse remembers how Snake beat him in the calendar race, so despite an initial attraction, these two could be wary of each other. Snake is impressed by Horse's energy and athleticism while Horse admires Snake's elegance and charm. Yet they don't really have much in common. Deep thinking Snake could find Horse rather shallow, and Horse may see Snake as frustratingly enigmatic.

Horse Love 2023 Style

Can there be any single Horses from 2022 still single? You were so hot last year, Horse; such a splendid sight as you sauntered your gorgeous path through every crowd... you probably had to fight off admirers in all directions.

Maybe you were so spoiled for choice you ended up choosing no one, permanently. You preferred a pick-and-mix approach.

Well, whatever the reason, single Horses are set for a replay this year. Your magnificence is only increasing, and you can't fail to turn heads wherever you go.

Yet, unlike the roaming Tiger, Rabbit influence is very family-oriented and home-loving. Despite the temptations, many single Horses will suddenly find themselves unusually keen to stop wandering and settle down.

The emotional Water element could even make you a bit sloppy and sentimental, Horse. Just hang on to that credit card on Valentine's Day.

Attached Horses could find themselves struggling with similar unfamiliar emotions. Long relationships could take on a roller-coaster sensation. One minute, a break-up looks inevitable; the next, you're packing for that second honeymoon. And then, of course, many a Horse couple will discover this is the perfect year to welcome a baby foal.

Secrets of Success in 2023

With everything turning out so well, Horse, you've probably not given much thought to improving your chances of success this year. For some equines, it must seem like all you have to do is get out of bed.

Well, that's a good start, of course, but though the Rabbit is not the strictest of bosses, Rabbit energy still insists on genuine effort being made.

It's quite difficult for the typical Horse to actually keep still and concentrate for long periods, so the Rabbit will reward improvements in focus.

The more self-discipline you can dredge up, Horse, the more successful you will be. Resist the urge to trot out for another snack whenever the going gets dull; force yourself to carry on even if you're bored, and you'll be amazed at the difference it will make.

Then there's all that lovely cash flowing in. Horse just loves to help it flow out again. It needs no assistance, Horse, so leave it alone.

This year, beware of unscrupulous types lurking around you, plotting ways of parting you from your savings. The sharks have scented your good fortune, Horse, and they're closing in. Don't fall for their lies. Ignore all unsolicited phone calls, emails, online offers, and salespeople. View all get-rich-quick schemes with extreme scepticism. Be especially wary of online lovers and sad people requesting loans.

The best plan is probably to hang onto your cash, keep it safe, and only invest in what you know.

The Horse Year at a Glance

January – It's been a good year for most Horses, but it's feeling stale now. You're eager for a fresh start.

February – Excitement builds around February 14. There's something special on the horizon, but will it last till March?

March – Romance is still flourishing, and work goes well. Are you popular or what?

April – The boss has earmarked you for a special project, or maybe you're the boss and you're planning something big. Looks exciting but check the details.

May – Someone is out to deceive you. Behind that charm lies something quite different. Don't rush in.

June – An early holiday, far afield, will work wonders for your morale. Go for it.

July – An arty friend is planning a party and wants your assistance. The preparations will snowball. You'll love it.

August – Work is going well, but a colleague or client drives you mad. Whether they're indecisive, or just plain picky, be fair but firm.

September – An attractive stranger catches your eye. Are they as delightful on the inside as the outside? Only time will tell.

October – A special friend drops in and suddenly the two of you are planning a partnership. Could be promising.

November – The cash has been rolling in, and you're tempted to spend, spend, spend. Resist all but a little treat. Christmas is coming.

December – And here it is. The festivities you love. You'll be reconnecting with long-lost family this year.

Lucky colours for 2023: Cobalt blue, Silver, Yellow

Lucky numbers for 2023: 9, 3, 1

CHAPTER 6: THE GOAT

Goat Years

17 February 1931 – 5 February 1932

5 February 1943 – 24 January 1944

24 January 1955 – 11 February 1956

9 February 1967 – 29 January 1968

28 January 1979 – 15 February 1980

15 February 1991 – 3 February 1992

1 February 2003 – 21 January 2004

19 February 2015 – 7 February 2016

6 February 2027 – 25 January 2028

Natural Element: Fire

Will 2023 be a Golden Year for the Goat?

Good news, Goat. It looks as if 2023 has the makings of an excellent year for you. Truly golden years look a bit different for the easy-going Goat than for certain other signs, of course. For a start, the Goat is just not the cut-throat ambitious type. Despite their reputation for being agile climbers, the zodiac Goat would be horrified at the thought of stamping over someone else to rise up the corporate ladder.

No, Goat would more likely be holding the ladder for someone else and cheering them on. Yet, oddly enough, Goat tends to do very well anyway, without obviously trying, simply by being so refreshingly likeable. People just enjoy having them around.

If you're typical of your sign, Goat, you probably had a rewarding year last year. Many Goats will begin 2023 in new locations or with more cash unexpectedly stashed away (than 12 months ago) than they would have thought possible.

So you did pretty well under the Tiger's rule, Goat. Yet, typical Goats – while appreciating their good fortune – would view the year gone by with distinctly mixed feelings. Tiger years bring change, often abrupt, sometimes shocking, and Goat finds such upheaval highly stressful.

No one would guess (seeing Goat's breezy, cheerful exterior and friendly smile) that the Goat constitution, while physically strong, is incredibly sensitive. In fact, Goats are the silent worriers of the zodiac, inwardly chewing over every tiny problem or unkind word. Upheavals, unpleasantness, or dramas – both good and bad – play havoc with the Goat nerves.

You may well have had more than your fair share of sleepless nights in 2022, Goat, despite other signs thinking things were going so well for you.

Well you'll be glad to know that though there are still a few surprises in store, 2023 is going to be much *calmer* for you.

Creative Goats will do exceptionally well. The Rabbit's tranquil energy generates the perfect atmosphere for Goat's inspiration to flourish and if you're not already marketing your works, Goat, you're going to have to start this year.

Even Goats that protest they have no artistic spark whatsoever will find themselves drawn to creating beautiful gardens, stylish homes, or eye-catching outfits that inspire compliments wherever they go.

This auspicious outlook is down to the fact the Goat and the Rabbit ruler of the year are great friends. You both share the same outlook on life. Rabbit is even less of a fan of dramas than you are, Goat, and you both long for serenity and a smooth path – which is what the Rabbit is aiming to provide.

Then there's the fact the Goat belongs to the Fire family of zodiac creatures while the Rabbit is a Wood animal. This means that, symbolically, Wood feeds Fire and helps it grow. In everyday life, this helpful relationship plays out in the form of Rabbit wafting opportunities your way all year, Goat, along with helpful people turning up at just the right moment should you encounter any difficulties.

The only thing to remember is this relationship isn't quite a two-way street. Wood constantly feeding Fire can get very tiring for Wood. So the sensible Goat will avoid overtaxing Rabbit's energy.

The secret is to think small but immaculate. Goats hoping to launch their own business can expect success as long as they start modestly and aim for gentle but sustained growth – the way Rabbit likes it.

Grand gestures may exhaust Rabbit's capabilities, so ditch lavish plans, keep everything low-key, good quality, and amicable. Then stand back and watch the venture gradually develop strong roots, unfurl, and blossom into wonderfully vigorous life.

Employed Goats, on the other hand, will find themselves even more appreciated than usual. Your opinions and ideas receive much praise and some sort of pay rise is almost certain.

This is partly because, like last year, the element of 2023 is once again Water. Water has the happy knack of washing cash into your bank account and friends to your door – though opportunities to spend it, probably aided and abetted by those same friends, could be just as plentiful.

Group activities of all kinds will prove very fortunate; whether it's amateur dramatics, evening classes, or helping out at the local carnival; the Goat will benefit in unexpected ways.

And, once again, travel is indicated. You don't mind too much where you go, Goat, as long as you've got some pleasant companions to go with you, and this year it looks as if friends and relatives will be organising a surprisingly tempting itinerary. In fact, they may even be planning a surprise holiday for you. You're going to love it, Goat. Just don't forget to put on your amazed face.

What it Means to Be a Goat

If people born under the sign of the Goat tend to look a little puzzled, uncertain even, who could blame them? It's not even definite their sign is the Goat. Some authorities call their sign the Sheep. Others – the more macho types – have it down as the Ram.

The confusion seems to stem from different translations of the original Chinese word.

But what's in a name? Whatever you call it, the qualities ascribed to the Goat/Sheep/Ram are the same. In China, the sign is regarded as symbolising peace and harmony. What's more, it's the eighth sign of the zodiac and the number eight is believed to be a very lucky number, associated as it is with growth and prosperity.

So, all you confused Goats out there can relax in the knowledge you were born in a lucky year.

In truth, perhaps the gentle sheep – the living animal that is – does resemble the zodiac Goat more than the real-life goat. Flesh and blood goats tend to have a feisty, combative quality and a strongly stubborn streak. Those sharp, pointy horns and all that head-butting does tend to put people off.

Yet, people born in a Goat year are known as the sweetest and friendliest of all the signs. They possess no spikey quality at all. They are tolerant and kind, have no wish to be competitive, and want to see the best in everyone they meet. Though they may not realise it, this attitude often unconsciously brings out the best in others, so the Goat's expectations are usually fulfilled.

Goats seem to get on with almost everyone, even people that others can't abide.

What's more, Goats usually possess a wonderful artistic talent. Even those Goats who feel they can't paint, draw, or manage anything skilled, are nevertheless immensely creative with a fine eye for colour and design.

The Goat loves beautiful things and even sees beauty in objects and places that hold no appeal for others. They love to use their hands in their spare time, ideally making something practical yet decorative. Knitting, card-making, cake-decorating, gardening, or renovating old furniture, even DIY, will give them great pleasure.

Concepts such as time and also money, have little meaning for the Goat. When the Goat gets lost in inspiration, hours pass in seconds and Goat ends up late for anything else that might have been on the agenda.

Similarly, money is frustrating for the Goat. Goats are not materialistic; neither are they particularly ambitious in a worldly way. Objects other people regard as status symbols hold little Goat appeal so they can't see the point of putting in a lot of energy to acquire them. For this reason, Goats are not career-driven. All they really want to do is pursue their artistic project or latest interest. If this won't provide an income though, they'll do their best at whatever job turns up, in order to get back to their true vocation at weekends.

The perfect scenario for the Goat would be a big win on the lottery, so they never have to waste time on a conventional job again. Should this ever happen, they'd be advised to get someone else to look after the funds for them; Goats are not good at handling finances, and the windfall could slip through their fingers with distressing speed.

Goats are notoriously impractical with matters such as bills, household repairs, filling in forms, and meeting deadlines. They just can't seem to find the time to tackle such mundane items. Though they're intelligent people, they'll frequently claim not to understand such things. The truth is, of course, the ultra-creative Goat brain just can't be bothered.

One thing Goats do have in common with the flesh and blood animal is their stubborn streak. Despite that easy-going, sunny nature, zodiac Goats can astonish their friends by suddenly digging in their heels over what looks to others like a trivial matter of very little importance. Once Goat has adopted this position, it will not budge, no matter how unreasonable or how poor the outcome is likely to be.

The Goat home is an intriguing place. Striking and original, it's likely to be filled with mismatched treasures Goat has picked up along the way. Goats love car boot sales, junk shops, and galleries. They enjoy beach-combing and collecting branches and broken wood on country walks. They've even been known to 'rescue' items from rubbish skips. Somehow, Goat manages to weave together the most unpromising items to create a pleasing effect.

Best Jobs for Goat

Potter

Party Planner

Beauty Therapist

Upholsterer

Teacher

Counsellor

Perfect Partners

Cupid's arrow can strike anywhere at any time, of course, but once the novelty of new romance wears off, some relationships are easier to maintain than others. Here's a guide to the Goat's compatibility with other signs.

Goat with Goat

When things are going well, you won't find a happier couple than two Goats. They are perfectly in tune with each other's creative natures and understand when to do things together and when to step back and give the other space. And since they both share the same interests, their together times are always fun. Yet, when practical problems arise, neither can easily cope. With a helpful friend on speed-dial, this would work.

Goat with Monkey

Monkey and Goat are different but in a good way. Though they don't quite 'get' each other deep down, Goat admires Monkey's lively personality and magical ability to come up with solutions for everything, while curious Monkey enjoys Goat's knowledge of the arts and the unusual. Long-term, Goat might not present enough of a challenge for Monkey but, with effort, it's a promising match.

Goat with Rooster

Peaceful Goat is not one to make feathers fly, so these two are unlikely to fall out, but they're unlikely to find perfect compatibility either. Goat is unable to give Rooster the regular ego boosts that make Rooster thrive while Rooster is baffled by Goat's unpredictable devotion to impractical projects or people. Misunderstandings are likely.

Goat with Dog

This is another relationship that could be tricky. Loyal Dog would be quite willing to stand by Goat when practical problems loom but could end up irritated by Goat's inability to learn from previous mistakes and so keeps making them. Goat can't understand why Dog gets so bothered. With care, these two could learn to live together.

Goat with Pig

Happy-go-lucky Pig and laid-back Goat make a good pair. They hate to stir up trouble and always look for a peaceful solution to any challenge. Ideally, they'd avoid the challenge altogether. They could be very contented together as long as Pig's spending and Goat's inability to deal with finances doesn't get them into trouble.

Goat with Rat

The Rat is charmed by carefree Goat and fascinated by its artistic talent and happy knack of living in the present. Easy-going Goat tends to like everyone so is perfectly content to enjoy Rat's company. These two can get along fine, yet they don't really understand each other deep down. Long-term, the Rat may find Goat's lack of interest in the practical side of life irritating.

Goat with Ox

Though these two share artistic natures (even if in the case of the Ox, they're well hidden), deep down they don't 'get' one another. Ox may be beguiled at first by Goat's friendly, easy-going manner but then disappointed to discover Goat seems to find everyone equally delightful, even those who are plainly unworthy. Goat, on the other hand, can't understand why Ox won't lighten up more. This relationship would require a lot of effort and compromise.

Goat with Tiger

Tiger and Goat don't have a lot in common. While their aims and temperaments are quite different, they are both sociable creatures and Goat wouldn't mind Tiger attracting all the attention when they're out together. Tiger, in return, would appreciate Goat's lack of jealousy and generosity of spirit. Yet, long-term, they're likely to drift apart as they follow their different interests.

Goat with Rabbit

Wow! One glance across a crowded room and that's it for Goat and Rabbit. Rabbit instantly recognises and appreciates Goat's innate style and authenticity, while Goat admires Rabbit's restrained elegance and understated intellect. Both quiet, home-loving types, they also adore exploring and acquiring fine things. This couple will never be bored.

Goat with Dragon

Goat tends to baffle the busy Dragon. Dragon can see Goat is the creative type but can't understand why Goat doesn't appear to be working very hard when so much could be achieved. In fact, if they stayed together long enough, Dragon could help Goat make the most of many talents but it's unlikely either of them can sustain enough interest for this to happen.

Goat with Snake

Snake and Goat could enjoy many happy hours touring art galleries and exhibitions together. Neither of them craves excitement and harsh, adrenaline-boosting activities and both appreciate creative, artistic personalities. There's no pressure to compete with each other so these two would sail along quite contentedly. Not a passionate alliance but they could be happy.

Goat with Horse

Goat and Horse just click! These two love kicking up their heels and trotting off into the green. Goat doesn't need to go far or do anything strenuous but is always up for a break in routine, while Horse doesn't do routine at all so is constantly on the lookout for a partner ready to escape. This couple rarely considers the consequences, but mostly, they don't need to.

Goat Love 2023 Style

Your love life is not going to be boring this year if you're a single Goat. For a start, Goats always get themselves noticed, which is odd because that's never their intention. If you're a typical Goat, you prefer to sidle discreetly into gatherings, hugging the wall and not pushing yourself forward in any way.

Maybe it's that dayglo purple and lime green sweater you threw on (because the contrast pleased you) or the unusual thing you did with your hair (blue spikes with silver glitter anyone?) but, somehow, despite your best efforts, you end up centre of attention.

This year, the single Goat, not looking for love at all, accidentally stumbles across romance while pursuing a new interest or hobby. Whether it's archaeology evening classes, joining a historical re-enactment group, or singing in the local rock choir, many a single Goat will meet their soul mate.

Just don't get too carried away too soon. Not all signs are as sincere as you, Goat. Don't commit until you know them a little better.

Attached Goats need to pay more attention to their partners this year. Long term love can be sweet in 2023, but there's also a chance your beloved feels a little taken for granted after certain events from last year. Time to dream up some little treats or splurge on a weekend break or three.

Secrets of Success in 2023

You're actually well set up for success, Goat, after what should have been a productive year with the Tiger, even if it wasn't particularly enjoyable at the time.

Now, all you need to do is carry on carrying on, plus make a few tweaks here and there to adapt to the Rabbit's way. This should come easily to you, Goat, as Rabbit's way is very like Goat's way.

The Rabbit demands perhaps more attention to detail than you're completely comfortable with, and certainly more care over budgetary matters, but if you can be disciplined with your spending and force yourself to tidy up those loose ends before dashing onto that exciting new project, you'll do well.

Perhaps most important of all is to work slowly and steadily. Pace yourself. You always like to do a good job, Goat, but Rabbit insists on the highest possible quality. This is the year to refine and pursue excellence. Do that, Goat, and you'll surprise even yourself with the wonder of your own brilliance.

The Goat Year at a Glance

January – Things have been slowing down which is a welcome relief in many ways. Take some time to relax and recharge your batteries.

February – An awkward character is causing controversy at work. You can sweet talk them when no one else can. Prepare to save the day.

March – You're flavour of the month due to your recent diplomatic triumph. Feel free to bask in everyone's adulation.

April – Spring is in the air and you're keen to get out hunting for new treasures. Don't forget your resolution about spending....

May – An artistic friend has a project to discuss. Do you want to get involved or are you better concentrating on your own plans? Think carefully.

June – A best buddy from the past invites you on a trip. Can you spare the time? You'll regret it if you don't.

July – Someone you met in a hobby setting is keen to become more than a friend.

August – Colleagues are on holiday but you're flourishing with a work project. Stay focussed. This could be a big success.

September – Whatever it was you were doing last month is spilling over unexpectedly into this month too – in a good way. Everyone's excited. Well done.

October – Progress suddenly stops when confronted with an objection – or an objectionable person. Don't give up. Work round the blockage.

November – The social scene is hotting up. You can feel that party season beckoning. Time for some strategic shopping.

December – Prepare for a festive gathering of the clans at yours, Goat. Think Santa's Grotto, Winter Wonderland... you can do it...

Lucky colours for 2023: Sky blue, ruby, white.

Lucky numbers for 2023: 2, 4, 8

CHAPTER 7: THE MONKEY

Monkey Years

6 February 1932 – 25 January 1933

25 January 1944 – 12 February 1945

12 February 1956 – 30 January 1957

30 January 1968 – 16 February 1969

16 February 1980 – 4 February 1981

4 February 1992 – 22 January 1993

22 January 2004 – 8 February 2005

8 February 2016 – 27 January 2017

26 January 2028 – 12 February 2029

Natural Element: Metal

Will 2023 be a Golden Year for the Monkey?

Well now, Monkey, are you in the mood for love? If you aren't at the moment, you soon will be. While 2023 has quite a few treats in store, the theme that recurs strongly throughout the year is romance and all the trimmings.

The first hint of what's to come could well appear as early as Valentine's Day. Either someone will surprise you with unexpected devotion, or you yourself will come over all sentimental and decide to spoil a beloved. Alternatively, in your cheeky way, you may impulsively send a naughty text to an attractive stranger — just for the sheer fun of seeing what happens next. And something will happen next! No-one's going to ignore you this year, Monkey.

If that sounds frivolous, then why not? If you're typical of your sign, you can be forgiven for a little frivolity in 2023, Monkey. 2022 turned out to be quite intense for you in many ways.

Though your finances probably received a boost and tempting opportunities presented themselves, many Monkeys found their good fortune was dulled by constant setbacks or unexpected problems.

It was all down to the fact the Tiger, ruler of 2022, has never been a huge fan of yours, Monkey. You don't share the same irreverent sense of humour, and the Tiger doesn't approve of the Monkey's weakness for practical jokes.

Fortunately, the Tiger is also renowned for a sense of justice so although it wouldn't exert itself to smooth your path, Monkey, it wouldn't deliberately block it either, especially if you were seen to be making a sincere effort to move forward.

Despite this, you can't help feeling Tiger likes to hurl challenges Monkey's way. It's in the vain hope of forcing the giddy primate to adopt a more serious attitude. As far as Tiger's concerned, life is no laughing matter, and you can take that silly Monkey smirk off your face right now.

Well, whatever Tiger's aims, you learned a lot last year, Monkey, and the good news is that everything improves in 2023. The Rabbit handles your affairs with much more delicate paws.

Like the Tiger, the Rabbit belongs to the Wood family of creatures, while the Monkey is a Metal animal. This is always a difficult combination since Metal is associated with sharp, cutting objects such as axes, which can do Wood a great deal of harm. Not surprisingly, Wood creatures prefer to keep out of Metal's way.

Yet Rabbit energy is tolerant and peaceful. Rabbit wants to help, and this year the Rabbit reckons what you need, Monkey, is a good helping of romance. And since Wood is the energy of growth, you can expect your love life to keep on flourishing and expanding as the year goes on.

The other element to bear in mind is Water, which is the ruling element of the year. Water will bring cash sailing into your bank account and work offers swirling into your orbit. It will also bring friends and relatives you've possibly not seen for years pouring through your door.

This is delightful, of course. Water is believed to be a great friend of Metal and is only too happy to keep flowing round. The trouble is it's not quite an equal relationship. Traditionally, Metal supports Water, so what is a fun association for Water can be a draining experience for Metal.

In day-to-day life, this energy could play out as an endless stream of visitors wanting to come and stay. Family and friends suddenly needing a shoulder to cry on, a baby sitter, or dog-walker at short notice, or even financial support to help them over the cost of living crisis.

You could end up thinking it's nice to be popular, but not that nice!

Yet, all in all, this should be a simpler, more relaxed year for you, Monkey. Your career may not be uppermost in your mind but money should not be a problem, and you can look forward to very happy romantic interludes – some of them abroad.

What it Means to be a Monkey

There was a time when we tended to regard the Monkey as a figure of fun. The creature's awesome agility, effortless acrobatics, and natural clowning made us laugh, and if they sensed an audience, the animals would show off shamelessly. Which, of course, only made us enjoy them more.

Yet, in China, the Monkey was credited with far more qualities than merely those of a born entertainer. The sign of the Monkey is associated with intelligence, justice, and wisdom. Behind those mischievous eyes, the Chinese detected a shrewd brain and ability to plan the best course of action.

Like their namesakes, people born under the sign of Monkey tend to be physically agile. They're quick-moving, quick-thinking types with glittering wit and charismatic personalities. At a party, the Monkey will be in the centre of the group that's convulsed with laughter. Monkeys love jokes and humour of all kinds, and if anyone's going to start entertaining the crowd with a few magic tricks, it's likely to be a Monkey.

While not necessarily conventionally good-looking, the Monkey's lively face and sparkling eyes are always attractive, and Monkeys have no difficulty in acquiring partners. The tricky bit for a Monkey is staying around long enough to build a relationship.

People born under this sign need constant mental stimulation. They don't necessarily expect others to provide it. They are quite happy to amuse themselves with puzzles, conundrums, the mending of broken objects, and inventing things, but they also need new places and new faces. Few signs can keep up with Monkey's constant motion.

What's more, Monkeys are not good with rules or authority. They've seldom seen a rule they don't want to break or avoid. In fact, it sometimes seems as if Monkey deliberately seeks out annoying regulations just for the fun of finding a way around them.

Yet, beneath the humour and games, the Monkey is ambitious with an astute brain. Monkeys can turn their hand to almost anything and make a success of it, but they're probably best-suited to working for themselves. If anyone is going to benefit from their efforts they believe it should be, chiefly, themselves. Also, they're not good at taking orders and, to be fair, they're so clever they don't need to. They can usually see the best way to carry out a task better than anyone else.

The Monkey home is often a work in progress. Monkey is always looking for a quicker, easier, cheaper, or more efficient way of doing everything and new ideas could encompass the entire building from the plumbing to the lighting and novel security systems. The first home in the street to be operated by remote control is likely to be the Monkey's. Yet, chances are, Monkey would prefer to meet friends in a nearby restaurant.

When it comes to holidays, Monkeys can have a bag packed seemingly in seconds, and are ready to be off anywhere, anytime. They don't much mind where they go as long as it's interesting, unusual, and offers plenty to be discovered. Lying on a sun-lounger for extended periods does not appeal.

Best Jobs for Monkey 2023

Jeweller

Magician

Chess Master

Croupier

Scientist

Museum Curator

Actor

Tour Operator

Perfect Partners

Cupid's arrow can strike anywhere at any time, of course, but once the novelty of new romance wears off, some relationships are easier to maintain than others. Here's a guide to the Monkey compatibility with other signs.

Monkey with Monkey

It's not always the case that opposites attract. More often, like attracts like and when two Monkeys get together, they find each other delightful. At last, they've met another brain as quick and agile as their own and a person who relishes practical jokes as much as they do. What's more, this is a partner that shares a constant need for change and novelty. Yet, despite this, two Monkeys can often end up competing with each other. As long as they can recognise this, and laugh about it, they'll be fine.

Monkey with Rooster

While not a perfect match, these two have got a lot of time for each other. Monkey recognises the intelligent brain beneath Rooster's plumage while Rooster admires Monkey's ability to entertain a crowd and they both adore socialising. They could enjoy many fun dates together. Long-term, though, Rooster may tire of Monkey's jokes.

Monkey with Dog

Monkey finds Dog intriguing. Monkey senses Dog's strength of character coupled with its playful streak, which fits well with Monkey's love of games. Dog, meanwhile, appreciates Monkey's energy and light-hearted approach. Yet, before long, Monkey's disdain for rules will grate on Dog's instinctive love of them. They cannot agree in this area, and it could lead to arguments.

Monkey with Pig

On the surface, these two might seem an unlikely couple. Yet Pig enjoys Monkey's fun and humour while Monkey is happy to be admired uncritically. What's more, Monkey's inventive mind can solve any difficulties caused by Pig's spending and since Monkey can't resist a challenge, the opportunity to retrain Pig, or at least find a way to obtain purchases cheaper, could help the relationship last.

Monkey with Rat

Unlikely as it might appear, mischievous Monkey and the clever Rat make a good partnership. Their quick minds, sociable natures, and love of novelty ensure that they're never bored together. True, Rat might sometimes feel that Monkey is too inclined to skim over the surface of things and could do with being more serious at times, but Monkey's ingenuity and audaciousness always saves the day. Both can have a weakness for gambling though, so need to take care.

Monkey with Ox

The naughty Monkey scandalises Ox but in such an amusing way that Ox can't help laughing. Monkey, on the other hand, is equally amused to find an audience so easy to shock. This unlikely pair enjoy each other's company and get on surprisingly well. Yet, right from the start, it's probably obvious to both that a long-term relationship couldn't last. A fun flirtation, though, could be a terrific tonic for them both.

Monkey with Tiger

Tiger can't help being intrigued by sparkling Monkey and Monkey is flattered by such interest. Who wouldn't enjoy being admired by such a fabulous creature? But irrepressible Monkey just can't help teasing, and being teased is not a sensation Tiger is familiar with (or appreciates). Unless the attraction is very strong, these two will wind each other up until they can bear it no longer and part.

Monkey with Rabbit

Mercurial Monkey doesn't really 'get' Rabbit. The Monkey can appreciate how well Rabbit operates and sees this approach gets good results, but it's all too picky and slow for Monkey. Rabbit, on the other hand, is amused by Monkey's quick wit and clever ways but deplores Monkey's slapdash, sometimes devious tactics. Very unlikely to work out.

Monkey with Dragon

These two are likely to hit it off immediately. Each is attracted to the other's intelligence and lively presence, and Dragon's exuberance doesn't overwhelm hyperactive Monkey. What's more, although they both enjoy being surrounded by a crowd, Monkey only wants to make people laugh while Dragon hopes to inspire them to a cause. There is no conflict, so this couple can help each other to go far.

Monkey with Snake

These two clever creatures ought to admire each other, if only for their fine minds and, at first, it's possible they might. But unless they're really determined to make it work, it won't be long before active Monkey finds Snake's energy-saving ways irritating, while Snake loses patience with Monkey's endless jokes.

Monkey with Horse

Uh oh – best not attempted unless it's love at first sight. Monkey and Horse have wildly different outlooks and can't seem to see eye to eye on anything. They're both lively but in different ways that don't complement each other. Monkey will consider Horse's moods illogical and pointless while Horse is irritated that Monkey makes no attempt to understand how Horse feels. Very hard work.

Monkey with Goat

Monkey and Goat are different but in a good way. Though they don't quite 'get' each other deep down, Goat admires Monkey's lively personality and magical ability to come up with solutions for everything, while curious Monkey enjoys Goat's knowledge of the arts and the unusual. Long-term, Goat might not present enough of a challenge for Monkey but, with effort, it's a promising match.

Monkey Love 2023 Style

Well, as we established earlier, Monkey, this is your year for love. You can't fail. The stars are aligned, the Rabbit is on your side and – right now – you only have to enter a room for everyone to immediately gravitate in your direction. They can't even say why your appeal is so intense; they just know they have to get closer. And closer still.

Being the naughty Monkey you are, single primates will be tempted to play a few games to keep them guessing but, in the end, who can resist a new romance?

It might not last, Monkey, though the Rabbit does like to see singles coupling up, but you might as well have fun while you see where it's leading.

Attached Monkeys may find themselves appreciating their other half more than ever this year. After the preoccupations of 2022, the more relaxed vibes of 2023 will allow you plenty of quality time together to rediscover why you originally fell in love. Your partner is likely to be as smitten with you as everyone else this year, Monkey, so take care not to make them jealous.

Secrets of Success in 2023

Clever Monkeys – which is basically all of you – will have secretly done pretty well last year. By keeping below the radar, and not looking as if you were trying too hard, you've probably made a surprising amount of progress despite the setbacks you dealt with.

The discreet approach will still work well this year, Monkey. It's not essential but the Rabbit loathes brash vulgarity. So think *restraint* on every level.

Yet you can still allow yourself some fun, too. Colleagues and clients will warm to your light-hearted suggestions and appreciate your jokes; as long as you keep your outrageous streak under control. In fact, introducing some gentle humour into the workplace could transform the outlook this year, and may turn out to be another secret of your success.

But chances are, though you'll do well with your career, your main thoughts are likely to be more concerned with success in love.

The Monkey Year at a Glance

January – The last few weeks of the Tiger, and you're glad to see the back of him. You can feel the mood changing for the better.

February – It might be cold outside, but social stars are burning and Valentine's Day is likely to be special in more ways than one.

March – Looks like you could be juggling two dates, or is that three? Don't forget, you've still got work to think about.

April – Looks like the boss has also noticed your charms. Or is it one of your clients? Either way, proceed with care.

May – Renovations at the Monkey pad are overdue. Start ringing around.

June – An awkward client is making things difficult. Patience is wearing thin. Maybe a colleague can take over.

July – Torn between two loves? If you're single, it's difficult to choose. If you're attached, you may be forced to make a decision.

August – Time for an extravagant holiday. You've earned it. Enjoy.

September – A fun friend or colleague persuades you to take part in their event. It's not your usual thing, but there's a surprising outcome.

October – Make sure you keep to the rules this month. Don't push your luck with parking places, speed limits or paying your credit card on time.

November – It looks like romance has taken a serious turn. Make your mind up time.

December – Like it or not, you're entertaining the tribe this month. Get everyone to bring a dish. Save your energy but enjoy.

Lucky colours for 2023: Dove grey, cobalt blue, gold

Lucky numbers for 2023: 7, 1, 5

CHAPTER 8: THE ROOSTER

Rooster Years

26 January 1933 – 13 February 1934

13 February 1945 – 1 February 1946

31 January 1957 – 17 February 1958

17 February 1969 – 5 February 1970

5 February 1981 – 24 January 1982

23 January 1993 – 9 February 1994

9 February 2005 – 28 January 2006

28 January 2017 – 15 February 2018

13 February 2029 – 2 February 2030

Natural Element: Metal

Will 2023 be a Golden Year for the Rooster?

Phew, Rooster, are you a bit shell-shocked as the New Year begins? If you're typical of your sign, 2022 was quite a white-knuckle ride. Looking around now, you can probably see the benefit of various difficult scenarios but, chances are, you wouldn't willingly choose to repeat them, even if they have left you better off in many ways.

Well, you can relax now, Rooster, because you won't have to. 2023 is going to feel like a comfy duvet in comparison. Now you can really get to enjoy the rewards you earned through all that angst.

Much of the uncomfortable atmosphere you suffered last year was down to the fact the boss of 2022, the Tiger – i.e. impatience on four furry orange legs – was determined to shake you out of what in Tiger's eyes looked like lethargy. Change was deemed essential, and Tiger doesn't do slow and steady.

Many Roosters have seen their careers, their homes, or even their usual social circles, brutally pulled apart, kicked around, and then restructured in an unfamiliar way.

The typical Rooster wouldn't like it – who would? Yet when the pieces finally settle back into their new shape, most Roosters will grudgingly agree the makeover works well.

Happily, for your nerves Rooster, everything is different this year. The Tiger has padded back to the jungles of the zodiac, and the Rabbit ruler of 2023 is – like you – averse to drastic upheavals. The arrival of the Rabbit spells a period of calm and a chance to get your breath back.

If you changed jobs last year, your career is going to accelerate in a manageable but pleasing way. The same goes for any business you started. Don't expect to conquer the world in 2023, but you can look forward to gently increasing interest in your work and growing profits as a result.

The main focus of 2023 is likely to be your family, friends, and relationships in the wider community. All these things probably slipped down your agenda last year as you dashed about trying to subdue outbreaks of chaos; it was like you were trapped in a cosmic game of whack-a-mole. There was no time for the people in your life.

Now the Rabbit energy of 2023 is encouraging you to redress the balance. As the weeks go on, many a Rooster will be inspired to reach out to all those neglected friends and family members. Informal get-togethers, parties, and visits will fill the calendar, but – more than that – you could be seized with a need to give back to the community.

Charity work, helping to improve the local environment, volunteering for the neighbourhood food bank, maybe even standing for a political party – interests that never occurred to you before, Rooster, suddenly seem immensely appealing.

Many Roosters could discover a talent for public speaking and end up becoming quite famous, not so much for their careers as the good causes in which they're involved.

The reason for this sudden burst of sociability has a lot to do with the fact the Rabbit of 2023 is the Black Water Rabbit – bringing the water element splashing into your life.

Traditionally in China, Water is associated with, amongst other things, money, communication, and emotions. Last year, which was also a water year, brought more emphasis on your finances. This year, under the softer influence of the Rabbit, Water is boosting your communication skills and sweeping countless opportunities to create links with others across your path.

Since Rabbit is also a youthful energy, many Roosters could end up devoting much time to projects involving children and young people.

One way and another, Rooster, you're likely to be just as busy as last year, but in a way that brings you much more happiness.

Yet don't imagine, Rooster, there won't be any space for a bit of Rooster time – a pause to smooth those feathers, buff those claws, and generally spruce up that glorious appearance which got a bit tattered in the storms of 2022.

Several enticing breaks are coming your way, possibly associated with friends or family, and you may also find yourself travelling on behalf of that new cause you've undertaken.

What it Means to be a Rooster

Colourful, bold, and distinctly noisy, the Rooster rules the farmyard. Seemingly fearless and relishing the limelight, this bird may be small, but he doesn't appear to know it. We're looking at a giant personality here. This creature may be the bane of late sleepers, and only a fraction of the size of other animals on the farm, but the Rooster doesn't care. Rooster struts around, puffing out his tiny chest as if he owns the place.

The Chinese associate the Rooster with courage, and it's easy to see why. You'd have to be brave to square up to all-comers armed only with a modest beak, a couple of sharp claws, and a piercing shriek. Yet, Rooster is quite prepared to take on the challenge.

People born in the year of the Rooster tend to be gorgeous to look at, and like to dress flamboyantly. Even if their physique is not as slender as it could be, the Rooster is not going to hide it away in drab, black outfits. Roosters enjoy colour and style, and they dress to be noticed. These are not shy retiring types. They like attention, and they do whatever they can to get it.

Roosters are charming and popular with quick minds and engaging repartee. They have to guard against a tendency to boast, but this happens mainly when they sense a companion's interest is wandering. And since they're natural raconteurs, they can usually recapture attention and pass their stories off as good entertainment.

Like the feathered variety, Roosters can be impetuous and impulsive. They tend to rush into situations and commitments that are far too demanding, without a second thought and then, later on, wonder frantically how they're going to manage. Oddly enough, they usually make things work but only after ferocious effort. Roosters just can't help taking a risk.

Although they're gregarious and often surrounded by friends, there's a sense that – deep down – few people know the real Rooster. Underneath the bright plumage and cheerful banter, Rooster is quite private and a little vulnerable. Perhaps Roosters fear they'll disappear or get trampled on if they don't make enough noise. So they need frequent reassurance that they're liked and appreciated.

With all the emphasis Rooster puts on the splendid Rooster appearance, it's often overlooked that, in fact, the Rooster has a good brain and is quite a thinker. Roosters keep up with current affairs, they're shrewd with money and business matters, and though you never see them doing it, in private they're busily reading up on all the latest information on their particular field.

At work, Rooster wants to be the boss and often ends up that way. Failing that, Roosters will go it alone and start their own business. They're usually successful due to the Rooster's phenomenal hard work, but when things do go wrong, it's likely to be down to the Rooster's compulsion to take a risk or promise more than it's possible to deliver. Also, while being sensitive to criticism, themselves, Roosters can be extremely frank in putting across their views to others. They may pride themselves on their plain-speaking, but it may not do them any favours with customers and employees.

Rooster thinks the home should be a reflection of its owner's splendid image so, if at all possible, it will be lavish, smart, and full of enviable items. They have good taste, in a colourful way, and don't mind spending money on impressive pieces. If the Rooster can be persuaded to take a holiday, a five-star hotel in a prestigious location with plenty of socialising would be ideal, or a luxury cruise with a place at the Captain's Table.

Best Jobs for Rooster 2023

Mayor

DJ

Teacher

Restaurant Manager

Referee

Fashion Designer

Perfect Partners

Cupid's arrow can strike anywhere at any time, of course, but once the novelty of new romance wears off, some relationships are easier to maintain than others. Here's a guide to the Rooster's compatibility with other signs.

Rooster with Rooster

Fabulous to look at though they would be, these two alpha creatures would find it difficult to share the limelight. They can't help admiring each other at first sight, but since both needs to be the boss, there could be endless squabbles for dominance. What's more, neither would be able to give the other the regular reassurance they need. Probably not worth attempting.

Rooster with Dog

Rooster and Dog are not the best of partners. Dog can be as plain-spoken as Rooster and is not likely to be impressed by overt show. What's more, Dog is often critical, and Rooster can't stand criticism. Rooster, on the other hand, is likely to sense and resent Dog's attitude. Frustration abounds for both in this relationship. Only for the hopelessly love-struck.

Rooster with Pig

These two might seem an unlikely couple – modest Pig with extrovert Rooster. Yet Pig has no need or wish to crow and can see the vulnerable character that lurks beneath Rooster's fine feathers; Rooster, meanwhile, responds to Pig's kindness and undemanding nature. As long as Rooster doesn't get bored, this can be a contented relationship.

Rooster with Rat

The first thing Rat notices about the Rooster is its beautiful plumage, but this is a relationship which is unlikely to get much further than initial admiration. Rooster's direct and frank approach can strike the Rat as tactless, while the Rooster can't understand why Rat has to make life so convoluted and complicated. Then again, Rooster's natural confidence and aplomb can come across as bragging to the Rat. These two have to be very determined to make a partnership work.

Rooster with Ox

For all its bravado and showing off, the Rooster is a down-to-earth type, drawn to security and accumulating the good things in life – requirements that Ox understands very well and can supply effortlessly. What's more, Ox can't help but admire Rooster's fine feathers and skill at communicating in a crowd – attributes Ox doesn't have and is unlikely to acquire. These two could enjoy a very good partnership.

Rooster with Tiger

The only feathered creature in the zodiac, the opulence and novelty of Rooster's appearance will draw Tiger like a magnet. What's more, deep down they are both quite serious-minded types so on one level they'll have much to share. Yet, despite this, they're not really on the same wavelength and misunderstandings will keep recurring. Could be hard work.

Rooster with Rabbit

A difficult match. However unfair it seems, Rooster comes over as loud, boastful, and uncouth to Rabbit while Rabbit appears dull, staid, and insufficiently admiring of Rooster's fine feathers to appeal to Rooster. These two just can't see below the surface of the other and it would be surprising if they ended up together. Only to be considered by the very determined.

Rooster with Dragon

A Dragon and Rooster pairing will always attract attention. These two are both gorgeous beings and love to be surrounded by admirers. They will probably enjoy going out together and being seen as a couple, but in the long-term they may not be able to provide the kind of support each secretly needs. Entertaining for a while but probably not a lasting relationship.

Rooster with Snake

Surprisingly, Snake and Rooster work well together. Both gorgeous in different ways, they complement each other without competing. Snake's keen eyes can see beneath Rooster's proud facade to the sensitive, unsure person inside, while Rooster appreciates Snake's unobtrusive strength and wise words of encouragement at just the right moment. These two could be inseparable.

Rooster with Horse

The eye-catching Rooster intrigues Horse while Rooster appreciates Horse's strength and agility. They can enjoy many stimulating dates together. Yet, in the long-run, this couple may not be able to provide the stability the other needs. They're both sensitive types but in different ways. After a while, the relationship could run out of steam.

Rooster with Goat

Peaceful Goat is not one to make feathers fly, so these two are unlikely to fall out, but they're unlikely to find perfect compatibility either. Goat is unable to give Rooster the regular ego boosts that make Rooster thrive while Rooster is baffled by Goat's unpredictable devotion to impractical projects or people. Misunderstandings are likely.

Rooster with Monkey

While not a perfect match, these two have got a lot of time for each other. Monkey recognises the intelligent brain beneath Rooster's plumage while Rooster admires Monkey's ability to entertain a crowd and they both adore socialising. They could enjoy many fun dates together. Long-term, though, Rooster may tire of Monkey's jokes.

Rooster Love 2023 Style

Many Roosters will have walked into 2023 as newly single – last year's Tiger having overseen quite a few break-ups. Yet, it was all for a good cause. The cause of finding you someone much better. And this year, Rooster, you're not going to be short of offers.

For a start, the Rooster is a magnificent sight, single or attached. And now you've got more time to treat yourself to some new clothes and restyle your hair, you're positively dazzling. Prospective partners will be queuing up, yet you're probably not about to rush into anything long-term, Rooster. After last year, single Roosters are likely to be a little more cautious about committing themselves. Which is fine, because now you can just relax and have fun. And you know what? By the year's end, you may not be a single Rooster anymore.

It could be just the opposite for attached Roosters. Many attached Roosters arrive in 2023 as newly attached. If that's you, this year gives you the space to establish your relationship blissfully. Long-term Rooster partnerships, on the other hand, are probably in need of some TLC. If you've come through last year and remained a couple – well done – but the relationship could probably do with some patching up and repair. Since your communication skills are at an all-time high, concentrate on getting to know your love all over again. Show how much you care and watch the relationship soar to incredible new heights.

Secrets of Success in 2023

So, maybe this year you're too exhausted even to think about success, Rooster. Managing to put one claw in front of the other may now be your idea of a productive day after the exertions of 2022.

Yet if you could just dump the negative attitude, you've got a lot going for you this year. It's time to spread those wings again and fly in a completely different direction.

The Rabbit energy is urging you on towards community service, joint efforts, and concentrating on the bigger picture for the benefit of all, not just the Rooster clan.

Efforts on issues involving good works will be swiftly rewarded, Rooster. The more you do, the bigger the rewards, and the more your confidence builds. Although you're not seeking it, this way fame (if not fortune) lies.

Stand by for possibly your most meaningful year yet.

The Rooster Year at a Glance

January – Treat yourself to a large G&T or beverage of your choice, Rooster. You've just completed a gruelling 12 months. Relaxing vibes help you slow down.

February – A misunderstanding with a colleague needs clearing up. The two of you could be great partners with this obstacle out of the way.

March – Home improvements are on your mind, and you're feeling inspired. Get several quotes or shop around.

April – The boss thinks you're wonderful. How did that happen? Keep on doing whatever it was you were doing.

May – A new romance or friend unexpectedly comes into your life. The two of you just click. This could be long-lasting.

June – Jealousy is bubbling around you. Is it at work or in your love life? Either way, tread carefully.

July – A friend wants to tempt you to a spa break. If that's not your thing, make an excuse but get away anyway.

August – Social stars are shining. Accept all invitations. Networking now will be unexpectedly rewarding.

September – Something you're doing is very successful. You're popular everywhere. At home and at work – everyone wants your input.

October – A face from the past gets in touch. The face is not happy. Do your best, but don't let them get you down.

November – Cash is suddenly rolling in. Don't go spending it all; unexpected expenses are coming up. Celebrate but save a bit too.

December – Long lost family or friends appear just in time for the festivities. Make some extra space at the Christmas table.

Lucky colours for 2023: Orange, Gold, midnight blue

Lucky numbers for 2023: 8, 7 ,5

CHAPTER 9: THE DOG

Dog Years

14 February 1934 – 3 February 1935

2 February 1946 – 21 January 1947

18 February 1958 – 7 February 1959

6 February 1970 – 26 January 1971

25 January 1982 – 12 February 1983

10 February 1994 – 30 January 1995

29 January 2006 – 17 February 2007

16 February 2018 – 4 February 2019

Natural Element: Metal

Will 2023 be a Golden Year for the Dog?

If you thought last year was good, Dog, just wait till you get started on 2023! Compared to most signs, you breezed through 2022 scarcely breaking so much as a fingernail – mostly because you're such great mates with the lord of the year, the Tiger; and now, to the envy of the rest of the zodiac, it seems you're almost as friendly with the ruler of 2023, the Rabbit.

Ok, so you weren't without a trouble or two last year. No sign ever is, but thanks to the protective influence of the Tiger, every minor worry turned out to be nowhere near as bad as you feared. You ended up in a pretty good situation… all things considered.

And now, here comes the Rabbit to continue where the Tiger left off; only in a more discreet fashion.

Business Dogs will enjoy an excellent year, and this is the perfect time to start a new venture. Employed Dogs are likely to be in line for promotion, and self-employed Dogs can look forward to increased demand for their services.

Property issues seem to be on your mind again, Dog, and if you didn't manage to find your perfect home last year, Rabbit energy may well lead you in the right direction now. There's even a chance you might find yourself looking overseas, Dog, despite being such a loyal home-loving type.

Perhaps you'll be able to persuade the rest of the family to move away with you – because you won't feel properly settled if they're not nearby.

Under the influence of the Rabbit, many Dog families will be on the increase this year too. A happy announcement concerning a new baby on the way could take you by surprise before 2023 is complete, Dog.

The only thing that could slow you down is the fact that this year's Rabbit is the Black Water Rabbit, so just like last year, the ruling element for the next twelve months is Water.

As Dog belongs to the Metal family of creatures and Water and Metal get along fine, this isn't a bad thing. It's just that Metal is believed to support Water – to play a nurturing role – and after being supportive all round for the whole of last year, you could discover your empathy reserves running low.

Water influences feelings, too, so you could find yourself surrounded by unusually over-emotional family members determined to cause arguments and make outrageous demands. What's more, any misunderstandings or unpleasantness with friends or colleagues in the past could come back to bite you now. If you thought it was all over, Dog, you could learn you were wrong.

In fact, at times, you might decide to take off on your own to get away from them all for a while. This is actually a good idea, Dog. They'll appreciate your calming influence and sensible advice all the more when you get back.

The other thing about Water is that it encourages cash to flow. This will have a wonderful effect on your bank account, Dog, but the same impulse also inspires you to spend.

Opportunities to splash the cash will sweep in, like the tide in 2023, Dog. You'll have to be very disciplined to ignore them. Enjoy the holiday of a lifetime by all means but try to have a little bit leftover for 2024.

What it Means to be a Dog

Though some cultures are quite rude about the dog, and regard the very name as a disparaging term, in the West, we tend to be rather sentimental about our canine friends.

The Chinese, on the other hand, while regarding the zodiac Dog with respect, discern more weighty qualities in the faithful hound. They regard the sign of the Dog as representing justice and compassion. People born under the sign of the Dog, therefore, are admired for their noble natures and fair-minded attitudes.

Typical Dogs will do the right thing, even if it means they'll lose out personally. They have an inbuilt code of honour that they hate to break.

The Dog is probably the most honest sign of the zodiac. People instinctively trust the Dog even if they don't always agree with Dog's opinions. Yet Dogs are usually completely unaware of the high esteem in which they're held, because they believe they're only acting naturally; doing what anyone else would do in the circumstances.

Since they have such a highly-developed sense of right and wrong, Dogs understand the importance of rules. Also, since deep down they're always part of a pack – even if it's invisible – Dogs know that fairness is vital. If there aren't fair shares all round, there's likely to be trouble they believe. So, to keep the peace, Dog knows that a stout framework of rules is required and once set up, everyone should stick to them. Dogs are genuinely puzzled that other signs can't seem to grasp this simple truth!

People born under this sign tend to be physically strong with thick, glossy hair, and open, friendly faces. Their warm manner attracts new acquaintances, but they tend to stay acquaintances for quite a while. It takes a long time for Dog to promote a person from acquaintance to real friend. This is because Dogs are one hundred percent loyal and will never let a friend down, so they don't give their trust lightly.

Dogs are intelligent and brave, and once they've made up their mind, they stick to it. They're quite prepared to go out on a limb for a good cause if necessary, but they don't really like being alone. They're much happier in a group, with close friends or family. What's more, though they're good managers, they're not interested in being in overall charge. They'd much rather help someone else achieve a goal than take all the responsibility themselves.

At work, Dog can be a puzzle to the boss. Though capable of immense effort, and obviously the dedicated type, it's difficult to enthuse the Dog. Promises of pay rises and promotion have little effect. The Dog is just not materialistic or particularly ambitious in the conventional sense. Yet, if a crisis appears, if someone's in trouble or disaster threatens, the Dog is suddenly energised and springs into action. In fact, it's quite difficult to hold Dog back. Dogs will work tirelessly, without rest or thought of reward, until the rescue is achieved.

Bearing this in mind, Dogs would do well to consider a career that offers some kind of humanitarian service. This is their best chance of feeling truly fulfilled and happy at work.

At home, Dogs have a down to earth approach. Home and stability are very important to them. They're not the types to keep moving and trading up, but at the same time, they don't need their home to be a showcase. The Dog residence will be comfortable rather than stylish with the emphasis on practicality. Yet, it will have a warm, inviting atmosphere, and the favoured visitors permitted to join the family there will be certain of a friendly welcome.

It's not easy to get Dog to take a break if there's a cause to be pursued, but when Dogs finally allow themselves to come off-duty, they love to play. They like to be out in the open air or splashing through water, and can discover their competitive streak when it comes to team games.

Best Jobs for Dog

Police Officer

Lawyer

Nurse

First Aid Trainer

Lifeguard

Kennel manager

Paediatrician

Perfect Partners

Cupid's arrow can strike anywhere at any time, of course, but once the novelty of new romance wears off, some relationships are easier to maintain than others. Here's a guide to the Dog compatibility with other signs.

Dog with Dog

Dogs love company so these two will gravitate to each other and stay there. Both loyal, faithful types, neither need worry the other will stray. They'll appreciate their mutual respect for doing things properly and their shared love of a stable, caring home. This relationship is likely to last and last. The only slight hitch could occur if, over time, the romance dwindles and Dog and Dog become more like good friends than lovers.

Dog with Pig

In the outside world, the Dog and the Pig can get along well together; in fact, Pigs being intelligent creatures can do many of the things dogs can do, so it's not surprising this zodiac pair make a good couple. Good-natured Pig is uncomplicated and fair-minded which suits Dog perfectly. Also, Pig brings out Dog's playful side – which delights Pig who's always keen to have a playmate. A happy relationship involving many restaurants.

Dog with Rat

The Rat and the Dog get along pretty well together. Both strong characters, they respect each other and give each other space when required. But deep down, the Dog is a worrier and gets anxious about unnecessary risks, while Rat just can't help sailing close to the wind if an interesting opportunity presents itself. Long-term, reckless Rat might unintentionally drive Dog to distraction. Only to be considered by Dogs with nerves of steel.

Dog with Ox

These two ought to get along well as they're both sensible, down to earth, loyal, and hardworking, and in tune with each other's basic beliefs. And yet, somehow they don't. Dog has a playful streak and finds this lacking in Ox, while Ox may be baffled by what seems like pointless silliness in Dog. If they can agree to differ, they could make a relationship work.

Dog with Tiger

While not exactly opposites, these two are different enough to intrigue each other yet similar enough in basic outlook to get on well. Both Tiger and Dog are idealistic and uninterested in material gain yet where Dog can be nervous, Tiger's bold. And where Tiger attracts controversy, Dog will be loyal. This partnership could be lasting and valuable.

Dog with Rabbit

Despite the fact that in the outside world Rabbit could easily end up as Dog's dinner, the astrological pair gets on surprisingly well. Dog appreciates Rabbit's careful, efficient ways and soft voice, while Rabbit admires Dog's energy and good intentions. Dog's lack of interest in the finer points of interior design might try Rabbit's patience, but with a little work, these two could reach an understanding.

Dog with Dragon

Not the easiest of combinations. Down-to-earth Dog can't see what all the fuss is about when it comes to Dragons. Unimpressed by glamour and irritated by what seems to Dog the gullibility of Dragon admirers, Dog can't be bothered to find out more. Dragon meanwhile, is hurt by Dog's lack of interest. Great determination would be needed to make this work.

Dog with Snake

Some snakes seem to have an almost hypnotic power, and for some reason, Dog is particularly susceptible to these skills. We've heard of snake-charmers, but snakes can be dog-charmers, and without even trying, Snakes can find themselves the recipients of Dog devotion. Since the Dog is strong, loyal, and can be fun, Snake is not averse to this but might, in the end, find it boring.

Dog with Horse

Both good friends of man, these two can make a formidable team. Dog understands the occasional need for solitude while admiring Horse's strength and agility. Horse, meanwhile, senses Dog's loyalty and down to earth nature. Both lovers of the great outdoors and physical activity, they'll never be short of adventures to share. A promising long-term relationship.

Dog with Goat

This is another relationship that could be tricky. Loyal Dog would be quite willing to stand by Goat when practical problems loom but could end up irritated by Goat's inability to learn from previous mistakes and so keeps making them. Goat can't understand why Dog gets so bothered. With care, these two could learn to live together.

Dog with Monkey

Monkey finds Dog intriguing. Monkey senses Dog's strength of character coupled with its playful streak, which fits well with Monkey's love of games. Dog, meanwhile, appreciates Monkey's energy and light-hearted approach. Yet before long, Monkey's disdain for rules will grate on Dog's instinctive love of them. They cannot agree in this area, and it could lead to arguments.

Dog with Rooster

Rooster and Dog are not the best of partners. Dog can be as plain-spoken as Rooster and is not likely to be impressed by overt show. What's more, Dog is often critical, and Rooster can't stand criticism. Rooster, on the other hand, is likely to sense and resent Dog's attitude. Frustration abounds for both in this relationship. Only for the hopelessly love-struck.

Dog Love 2023 Style

Another excellent year for love, Dog. Single Dogs may not have found their soul mate in 2022, but if you're typical of your sign, you had a lot of fun auditioning all interested parties.

If anything, you're in an even more playful mood this year, Dog. Rabbit influence lights you up and allows other signs that previously failed to notice your charms suddenly see what a gorgeous creature you are.

Outdoor dates, holidays in nature, parties under the stars, all will bring the single hound amazing luck in love.

Attached Dogs are ready for fun and games with their partner, too. The serious influence of the Tiger has evaporated like mist in the sun and attached Dogs suddenly feel like puppies again. There's no need to act your age, Dog. The two of you can frolic like teenagers and no one's going to say a word. You wouldn't care if they did anyway.

Secrets of Success in 2023

Success comes easily to you this year, Dog. The Rabbit is there to assist with whatever project you've got in mind, and you won't have to exert yourself too strenuously to complete the tasks you've set yourself.

The main point to bear in mind is that the Water element sloshing around could cause you to tire yourself, either by attempting to do too much or by forcing you to referee too many temperamental tantrums.

The Rabbit urges *restraint* in all things, so try to step back from taking on too many projects and from getting involved with fractious associates.

Also, take care to guard your reputation at all times. Dog is one of the fairest of signs, so make sure nothing you do could ever be misinterpreted as unjust or underhand in any way. With so many oversensitive people around this year, be extra careful not to tread on any toes.

The Dog Year at a Glance

January – You've hardly paused for breath, but you're not bothered. No slowdown for you.

February – Valentine's Day could last all month. Romance blossoms in every direction.

March – You're seized with the urge to spring clean – and that goes for everything. Think twice before throwing certain items out.

April – The boss or a big client looms large this month. You're not famous for tact but do your best.

May – A younger colleague or person in your circle could do with a helping hand. You're happy to help.

June – A friend has suffered a disappointment. Your generosity makes their day.

July – A move is in the offing. Either yours or someone close. Packing cases loom large.

August – A foreign holiday looks promising. You'll return here many times.

September – Keep a tight hold on your property. Thieves are lurking. Check your security and watch out after dark.

October. A loyal friend from long ago returns. There's so much catching up to do.

November – Someone in the family has overspent and it's serious. Will you help? Should you help? Can you help?

December – Lavish festivities in a new location, Dog. Chances are you're in the kitchen as usual, though!

Lucky colours for 2023: Red, Green, Aqua

Lucky numbers for 2023: 2, 6, 8

CHAPTER 10: THE PIG

Pig Years

4 February 1935 – 23 January 1936

22 January 1947 – 9 February 1948

8 February 1959 – 27 January 1960

27 January 1971 – 14 February 1972

13 February 1983 – 1 February 1984

31 January 1995 – 18 February 1996

18 February 2007 – 6 February 2008

5 February 2019 – 24 January 2020

Natural Element: Water

Will 2023 be a Golden Year for the Pig?

Well, Pig, it looks like you're putting the finishing touches to another culinary delight with which to welcome in the New Year. And in the unlikely event there are no guests to share it with, it won't go to waste.

If you're typical of your sign, you've had a good time in 2022 courtesy of your friend the Tiger, who happened to be in charge. And as the big cat departs, you're just as pleased to open the door to the Rabbit of 2023, who also happens to be a good buddy. What's not to like?

The great thing about being a Pig is you seldom have to worry about which animal has been crowned King or Queen of the year. The zodiac

Pig, while possibly lacking the obvious glamour of some of the more dramatic signs, has the happy knack of rarely antagonising any of them. This means that, across most years, the Pig tends to sail through potentially stormy seas to arrive on the opposite shore relatively unscathed.

But when one of your actual best friends has taken the helm, the outlook is even better. So it looks as if 2023 will be another cause for a Pig celebration.

The Rabbit and the Pig are always pleased to see each other. For a start, the Rabbit belongs to the Wood family of creatures, while the Pig is from the Water tribe. Since Wood, the energy of green plants, requires Water to grow, Wood creatures always love having the Water clan around.

On top of that, the quietly refined Rabbit and cheerful, easy-going Pig rarely disagree, so the Rabbit energy of 2023 will always feel supportive.

Rabbit has your back Pig, and after the boisterous atmosphere of the Tiger, the Rabbit aims to restore a little serenity to the Pig homestead. It also intends to inspire you to make more of an underused talent.

Water signs, while excellent communicators, tend to float happily about in so many diverting directions, they have difficulty concentrating on anything for long. Many a potential talent is wasted because the Water creature can't focus long enough to develop it. You tend to spread yourself too thin, Pig, and move on before you've finished the last project you started.

Well, not this year. The careless Pig attitude is incomprehensible to the Wood family. Wood creatures are dedicated to growth and spread. While the Rabbit wouldn't dream of criticising, Rabbit energy will nevertheless direct you gently to craft and develop that gift of yours and put it to good use.

This year, many Pigs will find themselves unexpectedly seized with the notion of turning a hobby into a business, training for additional professional qualifications, or even dumping their current career altogether and moving into a completely different field.

The Rabbit will help you every step of the way, Pig. Useful people will cross your path whenever you need them, the right funds will turn up at the right moment, and your applications will usually meet with success – unless, of course – unknown to you – they weren't in your best interests. Should you be taking any exams this year, you're likely to pass – though don't push your luck, Pig. Rabbit will still expect you to do the work.

During your career revamp, Pig, you may also be gripped with the desire to relocate your home as well. If you're typical of your sign, you probably have a great affinity for water and have always fancied waking up to sea, lake, or river views. Go for it, Pig. You could make it happen in 2023.

As the Black Water Rabbit rules 2023, the element of the year is also Water. This is great for water-baby Pig. You are literally in your element, Pig, but you have to take care you don't have too much of a good thing.

You can drown in too much water, Pig, and goodies can be swept away if you don't anchor them down while you can.

Stand by for a flood of tempting treats – opportunities, cash, new friends, a new home – but don't allow yourself to get carried away. This energy makes you emotional, and it's all too easy to become overwhelmed.

Keep your sensible head on, Pig, get a padlock for your credit card and you'll have a fabulous year!

What it Means to Be a Pig

It takes quite a confident person in the West to announce 'I'm a Pig' to an assembled gathering without embarrassment. Imagine the comments! And if they should happen to be at an event where food is being served, they'd never hear the end of the jokes.

Yet, if you were in China and came out with such a remark, chances are you'd get a very favourable response. You'd certainly not be a figure of fun.

The Chinese zodiac Pig – sometimes known as the Boar – is regarded as a lucky sign. Since flesh and blood pigs tend to have very large litters of baby piglets, they're believed to be a symbol of prosperity and plenty.

And given the Chinese fondness for pork, anyone who owned a pig or two would have been fortunate indeed.

What's more, people born in any Year of the Pig tend to be genuinely amiable types – perhaps the most well-liked of all the 12 signs of the zodiac. Cheerful, friendly, and lacking in ego, they have no enemies. They can fit in anywhere. Nobody objects to a Pig.

Pigs just can't help being kind, sympathetic, and tolerant. Should someone let them down, Pigs will just shrug and insist it wasn't their fault. Pigs tend to get let down over and over again by the same people, but it never occurs to them to bear a grudge. They forgive and forget and move happily along. Friends may scold and warn them not to be a soft touch, but Pigs can't help it. They see no point in conflict.

That's not to say it's impossible to annoy a Pig, just that it takes a great deal to rouse the sweet Pig's nature to anger.

The other refreshing thing about the Pig is that they just want to be happy and have a good time – and they usually do. They find fun in the most unpromising situations, and their enthusiasm is infectious. Soon, everyone else is having fun too.

It's true Pigs enjoy their food – perhaps a little too much – but that's because they are a sensuous sign, appreciating physical pleasures; and it makes them very sexy too.

Shopping is a favourite hobby of many Pigs. They're not greedy; they just love spending money on pretty things simply for the sheer delight of discovering a new treasure and taking it home. This sometimes gets the Pig into trouble because finance isn't a strong point, but such is Pig's charm, they usually get away with it.

Pigs don't tend to be madly ambitious. They have no interest in the rat-race yet they are intelligent and conscientious and can't help being highly effective at work, despite having no ulterior motive or game plan. They often end up in managerial roles. Their sympathetic and conciliatory approach, coupled with their willingness to ask others for advice, goes down well in most organisations and usually leads to promotion. What's more, while avoiding unpleasantness wherever possible, the Pig doesn't like to give up on a task once started, and will invariably find a way to get it done that other signs wouldn't have thought of.

The Pig home reflects the sensuous nature of the Pig. Everything will be comfortable and warm with fabrics and furnishings that feel good as well as look good. Items will be chosen for ease of use rather than style, and there will probably be a great many objects and knick-knacks dotted around, picked up on Pig's shopping expeditions. Pigs quite often excel at cooking, and the Pig kitchen is likely to be crammed with all the latest gadgets and devices for food preparation.

Pigs approve of holidays, of course, and take as many as they can. They're not desperate to tackle extreme sports or go on dangerous expeditions, but they can be adventurous too. They like to be out in the open air, especially if it involves picnics and barbecues but, basically, easy-going Pig's just happy to take a break.

Best Jobs for Pig

Children's Entertainer

Chef

Baker

Recipe Blogger

Event Organiser

Personal Shopper

Party Goods seller

Perfect Partners

Cupid's arrow can strike anywhere at any time, of course, but once the novelty of new romance wears off, some relationships are easier to maintain than others. Here's a guide to the Pig's compatibility with other signs.

Pig with Pig

When one Pig sets eyes on another Pig, they can't help moving closer for a better look, and should they get talking they probably won't stop. These two understand each other and share so many interests and points of view they seem like a perfect couple. Yet, long-term, they can end up feeling too alike. Pigs rarely argue, yet oddly enough they can find themselves squabbling over trivialities with another Pig. Care needed.

Pig with Rat

It's very easy for Rat to be beguiled by the Pig. Pig's easy-going, sympathetic nature immediately relaxes the Rat. What's more, Pig loves shopping as much as Rat so the two of them could enjoy many happy expeditions together. Conflict could occur through overspending. Pig does not understand Rat's compulsion to bag a bargain. Pig will buy whatever the price and the two could end up arguing over money.

Pig with Ox

Delightful Pig will catch Ox's eye, and since Pig isn't a constant thrill-seeker, the two of them could enjoy many peaceful evenings together, perhaps over a tasty meal. Yet Pig's spendthrift ways – at least in Ox's eyes – could soon prove very annoying as well as illogical to the Ox, while Pig could find Ox's attitude judgemental and upsetting. Not ideal for the long-term.

Pig with Tiger

Carefree Pig will love to bask in Tiger's impressive aura, while Tiger will feel good about protecting this charming but unworldly creature. They enjoy each other's company and Tiger, so focused on lofty matters, will find Pig's compulsive shopping too trivial to worry about. This couple could do well together as long as Pig's fondness for cosy nights in doesn't make Tiger feel trapped.

Pig with Rabbit

Pig is not quite as interested in fine dining as Rabbit, and is happy to scoff a burger as much as a cordon bleu creation, but their shared love of the good things in life makes these two happy companions. Once again, Pig's spending habits might irritate Rabbit, but not too much as Rabbit is quite willing to splurge on lovely things for the home. A relationship would work well.

Pig with Dragon

While Dragon and Pig might seem to be opposites, the two of them can create a surprisingly contented relationship. Pig is quite happy for Dragon to fly around doing exciting things as long as Pig is not expected to do much more than admire profusely. Dragon appreciates Pig's uncritical support and makes allowances for Pig's lack of stamina. This couple could live in harmony.

Pig with Snake

Pig and Snake don't have a lot to say to each other. Snake can't be bothered with Pig's endless shopping, and Pig is hurt by Snake's snobbish attitude. They both enjoy the good things in life so a luxury fling could briefly be fun – a shared spa break might be a good idea – but in the long-term, this relationship is probably not worth pursuing.

Pig with Horse

Pig and Horse are good companions. Horse is soothed by easy-going Pig and Pig is proud to be seen with such an alluring creature as Horse. They don't have a lot of interests in common, but they don't antagonise each other either. They can jog along amicably for quite a while, but long-term they may find they each want more than the other can provide.

Pig with Goat

Happy-go-lucky Pig and laid-back Goat make a good pair. They hate to stir up trouble and always look for a peaceful solution to any challenge. Ideally, they'd avoid the challenge altogether. They could be very contented together as long as Pig's spending and Goat's inability to deal with finances doesn't get them into trouble.

Pig with Monkey

On the surface, these two might seem an unlikely couple. Yet Pig enjoys Monkey's fun and humour while Monkey is happy to be admired uncritically. What's more, Monkey's inventive mind can solve any difficulties caused by Pig's spending, and since Monkey can't resist a challenge, the opportunity to retrain Pig or at least find a way to obtain purchases cheaper could help the relationship last.

Pig with Rooster

These two might seem an unlikely couple – modest Pig with extrovert Rooster. Yet Pig has no need or wish to crow, and can see the vulnerable character that lurks beneath Rooster's fine feathers. While Rooster responds to Pig's kindness and undemanding nature. As long as Rooster doesn't get bored, this can be a contented relationship.

Pig with Dog

In the outside world, the dog and the pig can get along well together; in fact, pigs, being intelligent creatures, can do many of the things dogs can do, so it's not surprising this zodiac pair make a good couple. Good-natured Pig is uncomplicated and fair-minded which suits Dog perfectly. Also, Pig brings out Dog's playful side – which delights Pig who's always keen to have a playmate. A happy relationship involving many restaurants.

Pig Love 2023 Style

The sexy single Pig has probably not stopped partying from last year yet. Every weekend is a good weekend to enjoy yourself as far as Pig is concerned, and why confine the fun just to weekends if it comes to that? Pig can find an excuse to celebrate every day of the week with some careful digging.

Single Pigs make friends wherever they go, and you're so attractive, Pig, those friendships often turn into romances. Few can resist the light-hearted Pig, and when the romances have run their course, they turn easily back into friendships. That's fine with the single Pig. Life's too short for hard feelings as far as Pig is concerned, and you can't have too many friends.

Yet this year, under the Rabbit influence, many single Pigs will drop the easy come, easy go approach. You could find your thoughts turning towards a more permanent arrangement. The Rabbit encourages coupling up and creating families, so 2023, single Pig, could be the year you find the One and finally settle down.

Attached Pigs, affected like everyone else by the Rabbit's youthful, expansive vibe, are likely to decide this is the perfect time to start a family or increase the existing one. Additional piglets, it suddenly seems, are just what's needed to make the home complete.

Secrets of Success in 2023

Anything that makes you happy, Pig, you tend to view as a success... so this year you won't have to make much effort. There's a lot coming your way to make you smile.

Nevertheless, the Rabbit is serious about guiding you to develop your talents or skills. If you insist on being lazy, the sky won't fall in, but in years to come, you'll regret not making the most of this very favourable time.

Any sincere efforts you adopt to improve your situation, to enhance your natural abilities, will be rewarded, not just in 2023 but in the years ahead. You will be amazed at what you're capable of when you really try.

But don't forget that in this watery year, your emotions will be hyper-sensitive. You're always a soft touch for a hard luck story, Pig, but in 2023 you must be extra careful. Unscrupulous types will try to take advantage of your charitable nature. Think twice before making any donations or handing over your credit card details. Better still, get a non-Pig friend to check out the cause you're intending to help.

Take care and this will be a wonderfully successful year!

The Pig Year at a Glance

January – The excitement's building. You can feel the new vibe in the air. You can't wait to get started.

February – Someone wants to spoil you. Maybe several someones. Don't fight it, Pig. You might as well accept... it would be rude not to.

March – Work romance could be brewing. Or is it someone you see on the way to work? Either way, the outlook's promising.

April – The boss seems to think you're not concentrating. This is possibly true. Get your head together, Pig; prove you're an asset.

May – Second thoughts about your job are occurring. Is it time for a change?

June – Second thoughts about your home, too. Would a different location suit you better? A friend helps you look.

July – A new course to do with your career could work wonders. Check out the brochures.

August – You've been talked into an unusual holiday. You have your doubts, but Pig can find something to enjoy anywhere.

September – An authority figure notices talents that were previously overlooked. Accept their encouragement.

October – An old friend reappears, and the two of you hit the clubs. A recurring theme this month.

November – Time to put in some serious shopping. Not too many days till Christmas.

December – Every year, you just get crazier with the festivities. Chez Pig looks like Santa's Grotto. You might keep the decorations up all year.

Lucky colours for 2023: Pink, White, Yellow

Lucky numbers for 2023: 4, 7, 1

CHAPTER 11: THE RAT

Rat Years

5 February 1924 – 24 January 1925

24 January 1936 – 10 February 1937

10 February 1948 – 28 January 1949

28 January 1960 – 14 February 1961

15 February 1972 – 2 February 1973

2 February 1984 – 19 February 1985

19 February 1996 – 7 February 1997

7 February 2008 – 25 January 2009

25 January 2020 – 11 February 2021

Natural Element: Water

Will 2023 be a Golden Year for the Rat?

Take a bow, Rat. You've cruised through 2022, skidded round quite a few tricky turns without crashing, and managed to arrive in 2023 with almost everything important intact

We expect nothing less of the wily Rat, of course, but if you're typical of your sign, your performance in 2022 was impressive all the same.

The great news is that after 2022, 2023 is going to feel like a spa break, Rat. Having used the dynamic energy from last year to set yourself up in a number of promising ways, you now get the opportunity to ease off a little and guide your projects to well-deserved success.

Last year was ruled by the feisty Tiger, another big personality much like you, Rat (only more so, if anything). The two of you aren't ideal playmates; you both like to be in charge, but your interests are quite different, so this can lead to disagreements at times.

What's more, Tiger's energy is even more formidable than yours, Rat, so you tend to exhaust yourself trying to keep up. The active vibe of 2022 suited your restless nature, but now and then you probably overdid it attempting to organise everything yourself and at top speed.

Fortunately, the Rabbit has shown up just in time to save you from yourself. 2023 presents you with an opportunity to slow down a little, enjoy your achievements, and soak up the admiration that's coming your way.

Recognition is yours in 2023, Rat, if you're typical of your sign. Whether it's at work, within the family or the wider community, people are finally realising what a brilliant operator you are. Promotion and pay rises could be coming your way in the next few months if your focus has been on your career, while if you've been pouring your efforts into your family or community, you'll be showered with gratifying appreciation.

The great thing about the Rabbit, as far as Rat is concerned, is that the Rabbit, while being a little wary of your outspoken ways, admires your verve and courage. Rabbit energy will support your choices whenever possible, only attempting – in the gentlest manner – to slow you down should you be in danger of going over the top.

Rabbit can't help looking out for you, Rat, because the Rabbit belongs to the Wood family of creatures and you are from the Water clan. Wood needs Water in order to grow. It can't exist without it, so of course it's in Wood's own interests to come to your aid when needed.

The other important point to bear in mind is that the element of 2023 is Water – we're welcoming the Black Water Rabbit, after all.

Since you're a Water creature, you instantly feel at ease in this rippling, swirling environment. Some Water creatures relax so completely when they're literally in their element like this, that they can get nothing done.

No danger of that with the busy Rat, yet there are other risks for the hyper-active rodent. When you relax Rat, you tend to let your guard down, which can leave you prey to con-artists, deception, and scams. So the Rabbit is urging you to keep that clever brain engaged at all times, even when reclining in the sun.

This year, many Rats will find that – as well as bringing them cash – the Water element is likely to wash a family member or close friend right out of your immediate orbit and away overseas.

Relocation to a foreign setting looks likely for someone in the Rat circle. Some Rats may not be too happy about this, at first, but if that's you, cheer up. Once you get used to the idea, you'll see their move opens up all kinds of exciting possibilities.

For a start, you can enjoy any number of free holidays – Rats always enjoy saving money – and you can also get to experience a different country like an inhabitant not a tourist (always appealing). Plus, you may stumble across all sorts of new business ideas that never occurred to you before.

All in all, their move could lead to a whole new chapter of life for the Rat. The upheaval is going to have very positive results for you, that's for sure. And, you never know, you might even decide to join them in years to come.

As a gregarious, family-loving Rat, you just love the bustle of parties, get-togethers, and just about any fun gathering. This is wonderful as, this year, the Water element sweeps endless social opportunities to your door, Rat. Possibly, literally to your door. Think house-warmings, bbqs, even street parties. It looks like your place has magnetic qualities this year, Rat – you're going to love it.

What it Means to Be a Rat

It doesn't sound so good does it, to call yourself a Rat? In fact, it may seem strange to start the astrological cycle with such a controversial creature as the unwelcome rodent. Here in the West, we haven't a good word to say about them. We talk of 'plagues' of rats; they 'infest' dirty, derelict places; they hang around dustbins.

They're associated with disease, rubbish, and sewers, and if a rat should be spied near our homes, we'd be straight on the phone to pest control. They make us shudder. Describe a person as 'a rat', and you're certainly not paying them a compliment.

Yet the Chinese view things differently. When they think of the zodiac Rat, they're thinking not of the flea-ridden rodent with the disconcerting long, hairless tail. They're imagining a certain energy, certain admirable qualities they associate with the creature. Rats, after all, are a very successful species. They are great survivors; they're quick, intelligent, tenacious, and they seem to thrive almost anywhere, under any conditions. All excellent qualities to be commended, if you found them in a human.

So, far from being an unfortunate sign, being born in the year of the Rat is regarded as a good omen.

Rats possess great charm and elegance. They're chatty, intelligent, and make friends easily. At parties, people seem drawn to them. There's something about their genuine enjoyment of being surrounded by new faces that makes them easy to get along with. Yet, they value old friends too, will make an effort to stay in touch, and a friendship with a rat is likely to last a lifetime.

Both male and female rats always look good. They believe that outward appearances are important. Instinctively, they understand that you only get one chance to make a first impression, so they take care never to be caught off-guard looking a mess.

This happy knack is easier for them than most because they love shopping and are Olympic-standard bargain hunters. They can't resist a sale and if it's a designer outlet, so much the better. Their homes are usually equally smart for the same reason. Rats have innate good taste and are as thrilled with finding a stylish chair, or piece of artwork at half price, as they are a pair of shoes.

They enjoy spending money and the challenge of hunting down the best deal; and because they're also successful at work, they tend to have plenty of cash to splurge. Yet, despite this, Rats can often be viewed as a bit stingy. They're not mean, it's just that Rats' strong survival instincts lead them to prioritise themselves and their family when it comes to allocating their resources. Within their families, Rats are extremely generous.

Rats also enjoy the finer things in life. They prefer not to get their hands dirty if at all possible and are experts at getting other people to do mundane tasks for them. They like pampering and luxury and lavish holidays. Yet, being supremely adaptable, they will happily embark on a backpacking trip if it takes them where they want to go and there's no other option. They're adventurous, and hate to be bored, so they're prepared to take a calculated risk if some place or person catches their eye.

Yet, this willingness to take a risk combined with the love of a bargain can occasionally get them into trouble, despite their super-sensitive survival instincts. Rats, particularly male Rats, have to guard against the urge to gamble. The combination of the prospect of winning easy money, the excitement of the element of chance, and the challenge of pitting their wits against the odds can prove irresistible. What starts as a mild flirtation for fun can end up as quite a problem.

The same could be said for suspect 'get-rich-quick' schemes. Though clever and sceptical enough to see through them, Rats are so thrilled by the idea of an easy gain, the temptation to cast doubts aside, against their better judgement, can be overwhelming.

But if any sign can get away with such unwise habits, it's probably the Rat. Rats are good at making money and handling money. They're also masters at spotting an escape route and scuttling away down it if the going gets too tough. Underneath that gregarious bonhomie, there's a shrewd, observant brain that misses nothing. Rats have very sharp eyes and are highly observant even when they don't appear to be taking any notice. They are also very ambitious, though they tend to keep it quiet. Dazzled by their genuine charm and witty conversation, people often fail to see that most moves Rats make are taking them methodically to the top. It's no accident they call it 'the rat race'.

Best Jobs for Rats in 2023

Salesperson

Tour Operator

Motivational Speaker

Business owner

Auctioneer

Driving Instructor

Perfect Partners 2023

Cupid's arrow can strike anywhere at any time, of course, but once the novelty of new romance wears off, some relationships are easier to maintain than others. Here's a guide to the Rat's compatibility with other signs.

Rat with Rat

These two are certainly on the same wavelength and share many interests. When their eyes first meet, passionate sparks may fly. This relationship could work very well, though over time the competitive and ambitious nature of both partners could see them pulling in different directions. What's more, if one should succumb to a weakness for gambling or risky business ventures while the other does not, it will end in tears.

Rat with Ox

Oddly enough, this combination can be surprisingly successful. Frenetic Rat and calm Ox may seem to be opposites but, in fact, Rat can find

Ox's laid-back approach strangely soothing. Ox is not interested in competing with Rat and will put up with Rat's scurrying after new schemes with patience. As long as Rat doesn't get bored and has enough excitement in other areas of life, this relationship could be very contented.

Rat with Tiger

The magnificent Tiger will always catch Rat's eye because Rat loves beautiful things, but Tiger's natural element is Wood and Rat's is Water which means that Tiger wears Rat out. What's more, Tiger's not interested in Rat's latest bargain, and Rat doesn't share Tiger's passion for changing the world, yet the attraction is strong. If Rat makes an effort to step back and not get in Tiger's way, they could reach a good understanding.

Rat with Rabbit

Rat finds Rabbit intriguing. Here is an attractive, stylish creature that doesn't feel the need to be pushy or take centre stage yet somehow manages to be at the heart of things. The Rat wants to find out more, while Rabbit is flattered and entertained by witty Rat's attention. These two respect each other but, over the long-term, Rat could be too overpowering.

Rat with Dragon

This couple is usually regarded as a very good match. They have much in common being action-loving, excitement-seeking personalities who hate to be bored. It takes a lot to dazzle Rat, but the Dragon's glamorous aura proves irresistible, while Dragon loves to be admired, so each enjoys being with the other. There could be the odd power struggle as these two are both strong characters, but the magnetism is so powerful they usually kiss and make up.

Rat with Snake

The Snake shares Rat's good taste and being elegant, sophisticated, and smart will delight Rat at first sight. These two get on very well on an intellectual level but perhaps are better as good friends rather than long-term partners. The Snake's love of basking in the sun for hours strikes Rat as lazy and dull, while Rat's need to rush around doing deals and meeting people seems pointless and wearying to the Snake.

Rat with Horse

Rat and Horse both fizz with energy and they love action and looking good, yet this is not seen as an ideal partnership. Nothing's impossible, of course, but these two will have to work hard to find harmony. The Rat will admire Horse's enthusiasm and cheerful approach but become impatient to discover Horse can also be fiery and emotional. Horse, on the other hand, can find Rat's risk-taking behaviour extremely worrying.

Rat with Goat

The Rat is charmed by carefree Goat and fascinated by its artistic talent and happy knack of living in the present. Easy-going Goat tends to like everyone so is perfectly content to enjoy Rat's company. These two can get along fine, yet they don't really understand each other deep down. Long-term, the Rat may find Goat's lack of interest in the practical side of life, such as finances and bills, irritating.

Rat with Monkey

Unlikely as it might appear, mischievous Monkey and the clever Rat make a good partnership. Their quick minds, sociable natures, and love of novelty ensure that they're never bored together. True, Rat might sometimes feel Monkey is too inclined to skim over the surface of things and could do with being more serious at times, but Monkey's ingenuity and audaciousness always save the day. Both can have a weakness for gambling though, so need to take care.

Rat with Rooster

The first thing Rat notices about the Rooster is its beautiful plumage, but this a relationship which is unlikely to get much further than initial admiration. Rooster's direct and frank approach can strike the Rat as tactless, while the Rooster can't understand why Rat has to make life so convoluted and complicated. Then again, Rooster's natural confidence and aplomb can come across as bragging to the Rat. These two have to be very determined to make a partnership work.

Rat with Dog

The Rat and the Dog get along pretty well together. Both are strong characters, and they respect each other and give each other space when required. But deep down, the Dog is a worrier and gets anxious about unnecessary risks, while Rat just can't help sailing close to the wind if an interesting opportunity presents itself. Long-term, reckless Rat might unintentionally drive Dog to distraction. Only to be considered by Dogs with nerves of steel.

Rat with Pig

It's very easy for Rat to be beguiled by the Pig. Pig's easy-going, sympathetic nature immediately relaxes the Rat. What's more, Pig loves shopping as much as Rat so the two of them could enjoy many happy expeditions together. Conflict could occur through overspending. Pig does not understand Rat's compulsion to bag a bargain, while Rat can't fathom why Pig is prepared to pay whatever's asked, but with compromise on both sides this could work well.

Rat Love 2023 Style

It's not difficult for the Rat to get themselves noticed. You're a highly attractive individual, Rat, but more than that, your personality is never less than sparkling.

You're not one of those boring types who looks terrific but has the conversational skills of a damp tea towel. No, to meet the Rat is to be instantly entranced. You're never lost for words, Rat, and as far as the single Rat is concerned, every year is a good year for meeting partners.

Yet, oddly enough, the Rat is not particularly fixated on romance. The single Rat will often let enviable opportunities for love slip through their paws because they're simply too busy to return a call.

This year it could be different, though. The less frenetic pace may make single Rats slow down enough to notice the delightful offer that's come their way. Your soul mate is waiting, single Rat. Open your eyes in 2023.

Attached Rats can enjoy a brilliant year just as long as their partner loves entertaining as much as they do. If the two of you are really compatible, you're going to have a fabulous time, hosting gatherings that will be the talk of the neighbourhood for years to come. If it's only Rat who's keen, though, things could get tricky.

Secrets of Success in 2023

It's more or less simple this year, Rat. Or at least it would be if it wasn't so difficult for you to do simple. All you need to do for success in 2023 is to *refrain* from getting in your own way.

You've planted the seeds; now you've got to sit back and let them grow. If you keep tearing them all up to see how they're getting on, you'll kill them, Rat.

The trouble is you like to be busy. You like to feel you're making a difference. Most of all, you like to be informed of progress, every few minutes if possible. You're forever tweaking and adjusting and embellishing.

Sometimes this approach is exactly what's needed, but not this year. In 2023, you need to trust that the growth you initiated is happening, at its own proper pace, and that interference will only slow things down.

For some signs, this advice would be a dream come true, but for the Rat it's torture. Rats love complexity, problem-solving, and an endless to-do list. So this year, Rat, why not take up a hobby or start a new venture to keep you occupied while your main project is developing? Just avoid get-rich-quick schemes… however convincing. Without doubt, they're all too good to be true.

The Rat Year at a Glance

January – There's a slowing down in the air but, for once, you don't mind. You can look back at your achievements with a smile.

February – The pace is picking up again. An authority figure has approving words. Pat yourself on the back.

March – An old friend has a gift for you. Some sort of celebration is planned.

April – Have you become famous? Suddenly everyone thinks you're wonderful. Whatever you've done, keep doing it.

May A snobbish person crosses your path. They annoy you but don't get drawn into an argument.

June – A special person is going abroad. You'll miss them but can't hold them back. Organise a leaving party.

July – Romance is stirring. You've got a choice to make. One or two or three? Keep the peace, Rat.

August – A foreign holiday is in the offing. A visit to the person who went abroad, or a combined business and pleasure trip? It'll be fun, whatever.

September – That awkward person is getting on your nerves again, Rat. Somehow you need to avoid contact.

October – An old school friend reappears. It's been years, but you pick up where you left off.

November – The office parties are kicking off already, but you've got work to do. Cut yourself some slack, Rat.

December – Last-minute Christmas shopping seems unavoidable. Great bargains to be had, though. Looks like you're the host this year.

Lucky colours for 2023: Emerald, Black and Gold

Lucky numbers for 2023: 3, 7

CHAPTER 12: THE OX

Ox Years

25 January 1925 – 12 February 1926

11 February 1937 – 30 January 1938

29 January 1949 – 16 February 1950

15 February 1961 – 4 February 1962

3 February 1973 – 22 January 1974

20 February 1985 – 8 February 1986

8 February 1997 – 27 January 1998

26 January 2009 – 13 February 2010

12 February 2021 – 31 January 2022

Natural Element: Water

Will 2023 be a Golden year for the Ox?

Well now, Ox, are you watching the dawn of a new year from behind the sofa with your hands over your ears?

It's not that you're a coward, just that you were probably hoping for some peace and quiet in 2022, and it didn't quite work out like that.

In fact, if you're typical of your sign, Ox, you probably did pretty well last year. Most Oxen saw money rolling in and work opportunities pile up in what should have been a satisfying way.

Yet the Ox is a sensitive soul, deep down. You're conscientious to a fault, and too many tasks tend to stress you out. Your responsible nature fills you with guilt if you have to turn jobs away, yet attempting to complete them all shatters even the Ox's legendary strength.

If 2023 is going to be more of the same – you'd prefer to opt out!

Well, don't panic, Ox. The Rabbit of 2023 has different plans for you, and you're going to like them. Yes, you're destined to do very well again financially – and also in your career this year, Ox – but the Rabbit achieves these miracles by guiding you to work smarter, not harder.

When you think about it, Ox, the Rabbit has had to develop some pretty nifty skills, which enabled the fragile bobtail to come a respectable fourth in the zodiac race, despite lacking your size, stamina, and muscle power.

So, in 2023, Rabbit influence will nudge you to think more like a Rabbit. Take a fresh look at your career and responsibilities. Don't just plough on; stop and consider how you'd tackle them if you weren't gifted with such awesome strength. Apply more brain-power, less brute force, and gradually some ingenious shortcuts will present themselves.

You'll probably find you can achieve twice as much in half the time.

The problem with last year, as far as the Ox was concerned, was the fact that the boss of 2022 was the demanding Tiger. The Tiger won't take no for an answer; it's an impatient creature that moves at warp speed compared to the ponderous pace of the Ox, yet expects everyone else to keep up.

Tiger believes Ox is a tremendous operator hampered only by a puzzling reluctance to hit the accelerator pedal. For this reason, throughout 2022, Tiger energy has propelled Ox on and on, in order to demonstrate Ox potential.

If you're typical of your sign, Ox, you've achieved a great deal in twelve short months, yet you're left feeling strangely resentful.

Like the Tiger, the Rabbit of 2023 belongs to the Wood family of creatures, while the Ox is from the Water tribe. Wood folk like the company of Water types since Wood needs Water to grow. There's no antagonism between you, it's just that Water creatures like the Ox can find Wood animal years literally draining, though they can't quite put their finger on why. This is what happened in 2022.

Fortunately, we're dealing with the Black Water Rabbit this year, Ox, so there's a lot of Water energy involved as well as Wood, which suits you better. Plus, the Rabbit is nowhere near as demanding as the Tiger. In fact, Rabbit never demands; Rabbit always asks, politely.

This means that in 2023 there's a wonderful sense of pressure being released. At last, you can enjoy the luxury of choosing your own pace.

Chances are, you did so well last year, Ox you can now afford to hire some help if you have your own business; or if you're an employed Ox, you could be getting at least one assistant to lighten your load.

Opportunities will still come rolling in, but *now* you feel free to pick and choose.

The Water element of the year will keep social occasions flowing along with work. But you may be perplexed by associates becoming unusually emotional. This may take the form of pleas for help – no problem for the practical Ox – or demands for Ox to understand their mercurial moods (a much more difficult undertaking).

There could also be an issue with a business partner or person brought in to assist you, Ox. Perhaps they've made a mistake, or perhaps there's an element of malice, but whatever the reason, you could find yourself called in at short notice to untangle a mess they've created.

Happily, it looks as if there are a number of holidays pencilled in for you to recharge your batteries. You may not have booked them yourself, Ox, and you reckon you're not that bothered by travelling, but one way or another, you'll be finding yourself chilling out in some watery spot – by a lake or an ocean. What's more, you'll come away feeling more invigorated than you have for years.

What it Means to Be an Ox

Okay, so hands up everyone who's secretly disappointed to be an astrological Ox?

Sounds a bit bovine and boring, doesn't it? The Ox might lack the glamour of the Tiger or the Dragon. It can't even boast the intriguing notoriety of a sign like the Rat or the Snake. In fact, here in the West, we may not even be entirely sure what an Ox looks like. Some sort of large cow, perhaps?

So, at first sight, you might be excused for thinking the Ox was dull. Yet, in China, that wasn't the perception at all. There was a very good reason the Ox was so highly placed – at number two – on the zodiac wheel.

The animal was revered as essential to country life. So precious, it was regarded as a gift from the Gods. So special, in fact, it's said that in the past the Chinese didn't eat beef. They couldn't possibly disrespect such an important beast by serving it up for dinner.

So, while the Ox may not seem as exciting as some of the other celestial animals, the sign of the Ox is respected and appreciated.

What the Chinese valued was the phenomenal strength and endurance of the Ox. Get an Ox moving, and it will plod on mile after mile, covering huge distances with apparent ease and without complaint. Without the work of the Ox, many a family would have gone hungry.

People born in the year of the zodiac Ox are believed to be blessed with similar qualities. For this reason, though unflashy and quietly spoken, they often end up being extremely successful in whatever they undertake – from their career to their favourite hobby, or creating a harmonious family that blossoms.

Oxen have a wonderful knack of planning a sensible, logical course to wherever they want to go and then following it, relentlessly, step by step until they get there, no matter what obstacles they encounter en-route. Oxen find it rather puzzling that other people can't seem to adopt the same simple approach. They don't understand why some signs give up before reaching their goal. Why do they waste their time chopping and changing and getting nowhere, wonders the Ox.

Ox patience is legendary. They may not be quick, or nimble, but they realise that slow, steady, consistent effort achieves far more in the long run. And the Ox is only interested in the long haul. At heart, the Ox is serious-minded, and though they enjoy a joke as much as anyone else, they regard frivolity as a pleasant diversion, not an end in itself.

Ox people are usually good-looking in a healthy, wholesome way, but they're not impressed by flashy, passing whims and fashions. Superficial gloss has no appeal. The Ox woman is unlikely to be found rocking extreme, designer clothes or wafting fingers iridescent with the latest nail polish.

Ox tastes tend to be classic and practical. They are instinctively private and hate to draw attention to themselves, yet the Ox is one of the nicest signs. Genuinely honest, kind, and sincere, Ox is ready to help anyone in trouble, happily pitching in to lend a hand without expecting anything in return. Yet, since Ox tends to speak only when they have something to say, other signs can find them difficult to get to know. It's worthwhile making the effort because the Ox will be a loyal friend forever.

What's more, when they do have something to say, Ox views can be surprisingly frank. Just because they are patient and kind, it doesn't mean they can be pushed around. The Ox is self-reliant and makes up its own mind; it's not swayed by the opinions of others. What's more, they can be very stubborn. When the Ox finally makes a decision, it sees no reason to change it.

Ox people are not materialistic. They work hard because the task interests them, or because they can see it needs to be done, and they will keep going until the project is complete. They are the true craftsmen of the zodiac, excelling in working with their hands and they can be unexpectedly artistic and innovative when the occasion demands. As a result, money can accumulate and Ox is not averse to spending it on some creature comforts. The Ox home will be warm and styled for comfort and practicality rather than cutting-edge design. If there's no space for a garden, it's likely to be filled with houseplants too, because Ox has green fingers and needs to see nature close at hand.

Travel and holidays are not top of the Ox agenda; they enjoy their work and their home and are not forever itching to get away. Unlike many signs, they cope with routine very well. And for all their modesty and quiet diligence, there is always something impressive about the Ox. Other signs sense the latent strength and power that lies just below the surface and tend not to impose too much. This is just as well because though the Ox may appear calm, placid, and slow to anger, when they do finally lose their temper, it can be terrifying. What's more, the Ox will never forget an insult and can bear a grudge for years. Ox doesn't stay mad – they get even.

Best Jobs for Ox 2023

Accountant

Doctor

Gardener

Teacher

Plumber

Ceramic Artist

Perfect Partners

Cupid's arrow can strike anywhere at any time, of course, but once the novelty of new romance wears off, some relationships are easier to maintain than others. Here's a guide to the Ox's compatibility with other signs.

Ox with Ox

These two could be very happy together, as long as one of them plucks up the courage to admit they're interested. Sloppy, sentimental romance is not their style and they both share this view so there'll be no misunderstandings around Valentine's Day. They know that still waters run deep and they can enjoy great contentment without showy declarations of love.

Ox with Tiger

Not an easy match. Ox and Tiger could be on different planets. Fiery Tiger doesn't frighten Ox and Tiger may admire Ox's strong, good looks and sincere nature but they both need different things from life. Tiger wants to dash about changing the world for the better, while Ox reckons you get more done by buckling down where you happen to be and attending to the details. Clashes could abound.

Ox with Rabbit

Ox finds Rabbit rather cute and appealing. Whether male or female there's something about Rabbit's inner fluffiness that brings out Ox's highly developed protective instincts. Rabbit meanwhile loves the Ox's reassuring presence and the sense of security Ox provides. These two could get on very well together as long as refined Rabbit can overlook Ox's occasional down-to-earth – Rabbit might say 'coarse' - observations.

Ox with Dragon

Chalk and cheese though this pair may appear to be there's a certain fascination between them. Ox may not approve of Dragon's showy manner but recognises Dragon's good intentions, while Dragon admires Ox's strength of character and gift for completing tasks. If each could find a way to tolerate the other's wildly different lifestyles, they might be good for each other, but long term, Dragon's hectic pace might wear even the Ox's legendary stamina.

Ox with Snake

Like Ox, the Snake is quietly ambitious and not given to racing around unless it's absolutely necessary. Ox, on the other hand, respects Snake's clever brain and understated elegance. These two could quickly discover how beneficial an alliance between them would be. They're both happy to give the other space when required but also step in with support when needed. This could be a very successful match.

Ox with Horse

Long ago, on many Western farms, Ox was replaced by the Horse and it may be that Ox has never forgotten and never forgiven. At any rate, these two, despite both being big, strong animals, are not usually friends. Horse is too flighty and frivolous to interest Ox for long, while Ox's methodical, careful ways will irritate the Horse. Best not to go there.

Ox with Goat

Though these two share artistic natures even if in the case of the Ox, they're well hidden, deep down, they don't 'get' one another. Ox may be beguiled at first by Goat's friendly, easy-going manner but then disappointed to discover Goat seems to find everyone equally delightful, even those who're plainly unworthy. Goat, on the other hand, can't understand why Ox won't lighten up more. This relationship would require a lot of effort and compromise.

Ox with Monkey

The naughty Monkey scandalises Ox, but in such an amusing way that Ox can't help laughing. Monkey, on the other hand, is equally amused to find an audience so easy to shock. This unlikely pair enjoy each other's company and get on surprisingly well. Yet, right from the start, it's probably obvious to both that a long term relationship couldn't last. A fun flirtation, though, could be a terrific tonic for them both.

Ox with Rooster

For all its bravado and showing off, the Rooster is a down-to-earth type, drawn to security and accumulating the good things in life – requirements that Ox understands very well and can supply effortlessly. What's more, Ox can't help but admire Rooster's fine feathers and skill at communicating in a crowd – attributes Ox doesn't have and is unlikely to acquire. These two could enjoy a very good partnership.

Ox with Dog

These two ought to get along well as they're both sensible, down to earth, loyal and hardworking and in tune with each other's basic beliefs. And yet, somehow, they don't. Dog has a playful streak and finds this lacking in Ox, while Ox may be baffled by what seems like pointless silliness in Dog. If they can agree to differ, they could make a relationship work.

Ox with Pig

Delightful Pig will catch Ox's eye, and since Pig isn't a constant thrill-seeker, the two of them could enjoy many peaceful evenings together, perhaps over a tasty meal. Yet Pig's spendthrift ways – at least in Ox's eyes, could soon prove very annoying as well as illogical to the Ox, while Pig could find Ox's attitude judgemental and upsetting. Not ideal for the long term.

Ox with Rat

Oddly enough, this combination can be surprisingly successful. Frenetic Rat and calm Ox may seem to be opposites, but in fact Rat can find Ox's laid-back approach strangely soothing. Ox is not interested in competing with Rat and will patiently put up with Rat's scurrying after new schemes. As long as Rat doesn't get bored and generates enough excitement in other areas of life, this relationship could be very contented.

Ox Love 2023 Style

The single Ox pretends they're not the romantic type. They don't believe in love at first sight, they say. They can't see the point in a string of relationships. They're not fussing about with the way they look in the hope of impressing someone. Such behaviour, in Ox's view, is all very shallow.

If that's you, Ox, prepare to be dumbfounded. This year, love at first sight could knock you sideways when you least expect it. And don't worry if you haven't been fussing about your appearance; it won't make the slightest difference. When Cupid's arrows strike, as they say, nothing else matters.

The single Ox is likely to discover this year what all those soppy songs were about. It will be a memorable experience, Ox, and you could find your life transformed.

The attached Ox should enjoy a happy year, too. If your partnership survived your workaholic ways and the stress of 2022, you're well set to reap the rewards of loyalty during 2023. The relaxed atmosphere will make you unusually sentimental, Ox, and you will delight your long-suffering beloved by whisking them away on days in the country and candlelit dinners. You'll end the year closer than ever.

Secrets of Success in 2023

With the Tiger out of sight, many signs will sigh with relief, sit back, put their feet up, and get stuck into the tea and biscuits.

But not you, Ox. If there's work to be done, you will tackle it in the same old way, at the same old pace, to the best of your ability, no matter who's in charge. This is why you can't help but do well. Consistent effort always pays off, and your honesty and integrity are appreciated even more highly this year.

Yet if you want something a little more spectacular by way of results, Ox, you should seriously consider overhauling your methods. As you know, the Rabbit is encouraging you to work smarter. Chances are there are many areas where you can update, try new technology, or pick the brains of more experienced experts.

You're not the most flexible of signs, Ox, you must admit, so you won't exactly welcome this suggestion. Once you hit on a way of doing things that seems to work, you tend to stick to it ever after. 'Why reinvent the wheel?' is one of the typical Ox favourite sayings. Yet there are times when a new approach and lateral thinking can transform your outlook, and this is one of them.

If you'd just drop the stubborn attitude, Ox, and go out of your way to seek innovation, you'll be amazed at your progress. You really will achieve more and earn more with less effort. Leaving you free to take on more work if you absolutely insist, or better still, enjoy some time off. What's not to like?

Watch out, though, as you power through with your ultra-efficient methods that some associate doesn't mangle the process. Maybe, under the influence of the Water element, they're overemotional and not listening properly as you explain the new system, or maybe they're just not up to it; whatever the reason, they can make life difficult for you, Ox.

Double-check their work. Keep a watchful eye on them, and everything will be fine. Go for it, Ox.

The Ox Year At a Glance

January – You quite like January. The quieter, pared-down atmosphere suits your mood. Enjoy the calm.

February – The pace is picking up at work. Someone tries to rush you. Avoid a tight deadline if you can.

March – Spring is in the air, and you're keen to get outside. An early break works wonders.

April – The boss has been stomping around upsetting people. You're not in the firing line, but your colleagues could use some help.

May – Someone special catches your eye. Have they noticed you too? Play it cool.

June – Do you have a rival? Either at work or in your social circle. Bide your time and observe the way they operate.

July – Friends or family, maybe both, are persuading you to take a trip. You're not keen on long distance, but hear them out.

August – It looks like those holiday plans are well underway. Don't feel you must work overtime to get everything finished.

September – They say opposites attract, and you could find yourself strangely drawn to someone who's not your usual type. Give them a chance.

October – Changes in the workplace. New technology needs mastering. You can do it, Ox.

November – Someone in the household has run up unexpected bills. Surely it's not you, Ox? Time for a budget overhaul.

December – You're tempted to downsize the festivities, but your nearest and dearest won't let you. Quite right, too. Enjoy the fun.

Lucky colours for 2023: Black, Yellow, White

Lucky numbers for 2023: 3, 6

CHAPTER 13: THE TIGER

Tiger Years

13 February 1926 – 1 February 1927

31 January 1938 – 18 February 1939

17 February 1950 – 5 February 1951

5 February 1962 – 24 January 1963

23 January 1974 – 10 February 1975

9 February 1986 – 28 January 1987

28 January 1998 – 5 February 1999

14 February 2010 – 2 February 2011

1 February 2022 – 21 January 2023

Natural Element: Wood

Will 2023 be a Golden Year for the Tiger?

Phew Tiger – what a year! 2022, that is. You've just climbed down from the throne, handed in your crown, and made way for the Rabbit of 2023 to take over the ruling business from here on in.

You certainly made your mark when you were in charge. We're not going to forget the Year of the Tiger 2022 in a hurry! So if you're feeling a little drained right now, no one would be the least surprised.

Strangely enough, though, rather than feeling deflated, many Tigers will experience an unexpected soaring of the spirits. It's not all fun and frivolity being star of the show. The role brings with it heavy responsibility and – in day-to-day life – this often plays out as a number of challenges for the ruler of the year to overcome.

How you overcome them will influence the course of your life for the next decade or more.

If you're typical of your sign, Tiger, you'll have successfully sorted any number of irritations during 2022, and now you're ready to wind down and enjoy what you've achieved.

You will get your wish in 2023. This is a great year for the big cats. While, in the real world, the humble Rabbit would probably make a light snack for the ferocious Tiger, amongst the creatures of the zodiac, the Rabbit and the Tiger are good teammates.

The Rabbit has been following in Tiger's footsteps for all eternity, a miniature shadow hopping loyally behind the big guy. The Rabbit wants to repeat your good works, Tiger, but in smaller, softer, more digestible form. Rabbit energy plays out like a distant echo of the Tiger roar.

For this reason, the Rabbit will bring you good luck, Tiger, as well as surround you with agreeable vibes. You and the Rabbit are both from the Wood family of creatures – very distant cousins as it were – so you just 'get' each other and instinctively help each other out.

This means that all those projects you started last year but didn't have the time or energy to progress as you'd hoped, will now lift off almost spontaneously. Whether it's your own business or a company where you work, ventures begun in 2022 will now blossom and lead to further opportunities which multiply pleasingly. Some of these opportunities could take you overseas.

Property may have been an issue last year, too – either you were hoping to move, or your home needed renovations. Unexpected hitches might have slowed you down. Well, the brakes are off now, and everything will fall into place. That perfect new residence will suddenly offer itself to you, or chez Tiger will emerge sleek and beautiful from its makeover.

Last year was a Water year, as well as a Tiger year, and the Water element is repeated in 2023. Water encourages communication of all sorts, and it could be that under the Tiger's abrasive influence, the communication that came your way was distinctly choppy. Family, friends, and clients were sweetness personified one minute, then demanding and unreasonable – almost irrational – the next.

Fortunately, under the soothing influence of the Rabbit, the Water element flows more calmly this year, cooling emotions and settling things down. Those same temperamental characters that plagued you in 2022 could now become placid, agreeable, and ready to compromise. In fact, 2023 will bring many happy family celebrations that will be remembered for years to come. Weddings, christenings, and red letter days of all kinds are on the calendar for typical Tigers.

Water also influences finances. Most Tigers will have seen plenty of cash pouring in, in 2022, but the stormy quality of the tide probably swooshed it right out again just as quickly. Expense piled on unexpected expense put a severe dent in many a Tiger's savings.

Once again, thanks to the Rabbit's laid-back approach, such extremes fade away, and you should see your wealth growing this year, Tiger.

Above all, the Tiger loves to be on the move. Last year, you probably had your share of travel but it was often marred by petty annoyances; airport delays, minor illnesses, lost luggage. This year, you can pack that suitcase with confidence. Don't be reckless, but with the Rabbit on board, your holidays should be carefree and relaxed. You've also got a series of reunions with overseas friends to look forward to.

You may no longer be the boss, Tiger, but you're going to love 2023.

What it Means to Be a Tiger

It's a wonderful thing to be a Tiger. Who could not be impressed with the great cat's magnificent striped coat, lithe yet powerful body, and arrogant, swaggering stride? We're all in awe of the Tiger – as well as being pretty scared, too.

In China, the sign is regarded as fortunate and noble. Fortunate because – let's face it – the Tiger owns the jungle and patrols his territory with savage grace; noble because it's believed the Tiger only kills when it's hungry or threatened. (Which may or may not be strictly true.)

Yet, the zodiac Tiger is also a contrary creature. You never know quite where you are with the typical Tiger. With a coat that's neither black nor orange – neither light nor dark – Tigers have two sides to their characters and can switch moods in an instant.

What's more, that striped pelt provides such perfect camouflage in the jungle; Tiger can melt into the shadows and become completely invisible, only to reappear without warning when least expected, to devastating effect.

Other signs instinctively know never to underestimate the Tiger.

Perhaps unsurprisingly, people born under this sign tend to attract good luck. They throw themselves into risky situations and escape unscathed, where others would come badly unstuck.

Tigers are fearless and restless. They like to be on the move and get bored easily. Wonderfully good-looking, Tigers tend to shine in company, and enjoy being surrounded by admirers, as they usually are. While perfectly happy in their own company and not craving attention, Tigers are confident and unfazed by a crowd. They take it as quite natural that other signs seek them out and want to hear their opinions.

The Tiger has a magnetic personality and can be highly entertaining, but they're also surprisingly moody – laughing and joking one minute, then flying into a rage over almost nothing the next. Despite this, the Tiger is very idealistic. Tiger can see what's wrong with the world and wants to put it right. What's more, courageous Tiger is quite prepared to get out there and put the necessary changes into action.

This is the sign of the daring revolutionary. The trouble is, Tigers can become so accustomed to getting away with audacious acts, they forget that – deep down – they're big cats and cats are said to have only nine lives. Push their luck too far, and sooner or later, Tiger can find it runs out.

Sporty and athletic, Tigers love to travel; when they're young, the typical Tiger is likely to want to be off to see the world. Even older Tigers insist on regular holidays and would happily take a sabbatical or 'adult gap year' if possible. Luxury travel or budget breaks, they don't really care as long as they're going somewhere different. They don't even mind going on their own if necessary, as they're independent and self-assured; they are confident they'll find an interesting companion from time to time, along the way, if they need one.

Far too individual to be slaves to fashion, Tigers of both sexes still manage to look stylish and original in a pared-down, sleek sort of way. They can't be bothered with fiddly, fussy details, and they don't need to be because their natural features attract attention effortlessly. Similarly, the Tiger's home is attractive and unusual: full of intriguing objects and trophies that Tiger has collected during their adventures.

At work, if they manage to avoid quarrelling with the boss and walking out – a strong possibility as Tigers hate to be told what to do – Tigers tend to rise to the top of whatever field they happen to be in. But contradictory to the end, the Tiger is just as likely to reach the peak of their profession and then resign to try something new. In business, the Tiger can be creative, innovative, and utterly ruthless to competitors.

Best Jobs for Tiger in 2023

Food Bank Manager

Reporter

Explorer

Vet

Social Worker

Environmental Lobbyist

Perfect Partners

Cupid's arrow can strike anywhere at any time, of course, but once the novelty of new romance wears off, some relationships are easier to maintain than others. Here's a guide to the Tiger's compatibility with other signs.

Tiger with Tiger

The attraction between these two beautiful people is powerful. They understand each other so well, it's almost like looking in a mirror. They both like to walk on the wild side and will enjoy some exciting adventures together, but their moody interludes could lead to fierce quarrels. This match could be compulsive but stormy.

Tiger with Rabbit

Surprisingly, the Rabbit is not intimidated by Tiger's dangerous aura, and this attitude immediately appeals to Tiger who enjoys a challenge. Rabbit's calm presence and clever way with words keeps Tiger interested, while Rabbit finds Tiger's adventurous tales entertaining. With care, these two could get on well together for years.

Tiger with Dragon

The two biggest personalities in the zodiac would seem bound to clash. After all, these larger than life characters share so many similarities there's a danger they'd compete. Yet a relationship between the Tiger and Dragon often works very well. They understand each other's impulsive natures, but they're also different enough to supply the support the other needs. They'd make a formidable power couple.

Tiger with Snake

Not the best of romances. These two are so fundamentally different that any initial attraction is unlikely to last. Snake likes to bask and conserve energy while Tiger wants to leap right in and race about. Tiger takes in the big picture in a glance and is off to the next challenge while Snake likes to pause, delve beneath the surface, and consider. It wouldn't take long before these two annoy each other.

Tiger with Horse

This athletic pair get on pretty well. They both like physical pursuits, testing their strength out of doors or just enjoying the feel of the wind in their hair and the ground under their feet. True, Horse may not quite understand Tiger's plans for world domination, but it doesn't really matter. Horse is happy to be loyal to such a charismatic partner. As they're both moody, there could be rows, but making up is exciting.

Tiger with Goat

Tiger and Goat don't have a lot in common. While their aims and temperaments are quite different, they are both sociable creatures, and Goat wouldn't mind Tiger attracting all the attention when they're out together. Tiger, in return, would appreciate Goat's lack of jealousy and generosity of spirit. Yet, long-term, they're likely to drift apart as they follow their different interests.

Tiger with Monkey

Tiger can't help being intrigued by sparkling Monkey and Monkey is flattered by such interest. Who wouldn't enjoy being admired by such a fabulous creature? But irrepressible Monkey just can't help teasing and being teased is not a sensation Tiger is familiar with, nor appreciates. Unless the attraction is very strong, these two will wind each other up until they can bear it no longer and part.

Tiger with Rooster

The only feathered creature in the zodiac, the opulence and novelty of Rooster's appearance will draw Tiger like a magnet. What's more, deep down they are both quite serious-minded types so, on one level, they'll have much to share. Yet, despite this, they're not really on the same wavelength, and misunderstandings will keep recurring. Could be hard work.

Tiger with Dog

While not exactly opposites, these two are different enough to intrigue each other yet similar enough in basic outlook to get on well. Both Tiger and Dog are idealistic and uninterested in material gain yet where Dog can be nervous, Tiger's bold; and where Tiger attracts controversy, Dog will be loyal. This partnership could be lasting and valuable.

Tiger with Pig

Carefree Pig will love to bask in Tiger's impressive aura, while Tiger will feel good about protecting this charming but unworldly creature. They enjoy each other's company and Tiger, so focused on lofty matters will find Pig's compulsive shopping too trivial to worry about. This couple could do well together as long as Pig's fondness for cosy nights in doesn't make Tiger feel trapped.

Tiger with Rat

Sleek and clever Rat can easily attract Tiger's attention because the intelligent Tiger loves witty conversation. Yet these two are not natural partners. Tiger's not interested in Rat's latest bargain and has no wish to talk about it while Rat doesn't share Tiger's passion for changing the world. Still, if they can agree to step back and not get in each other's way, they could reach a good understanding.

Tiger with Ox

Not an easy match. Ox and Tiger could be on different planets. Fiery Tiger doesn't frighten Ox, and Tiger may admire Ox's strong, good looks and sincere nature, but they both need different things from life. Tiger wants to dash about creating big changes, while Ox reckons you get more done by buckling down where you happen to be and attending to the details. Clashes could abound.

Tiger Love 2023 Style

You're stunning, Tiger. You know that. People tend to fall over their feet in their hurry to get a little closer when you walk into a room.

You probably don't even realise that, as well as your obvious good looks, you exude an indefinable something that draws potential partners to you. Even standing still, you radiate grace and strength; a combination lovers find irresistible.

So, the single Tiger usually has plenty of choice when it comes to partners. Last year was no exception. Yet, although there were a number of promising encounters, many Tigers found something went awry as the relationship progressed.

This was probably disappointing rather than heart-breaking for most Tigers. Deep down, the Tiger is wary of domesticity and tends to sidestep commitment at the last minute – without quite knowing why.

Yet, 2023 could be different. The Rabbit is a determined matchmaker and would love to see all singles happily settled in a cosy burrow. What's more, single Tigers learned a lot from last year's adventures. You've probably got a much better idea of what you *don't* want from a relationship now, Tiger – which makes it easier to recognise the right partner when they enter the scene. Which they may very well do in the next few weeks!

Attached Tigers could surprise their partners by morphing into purring pussycats in 2023. After the exertions of last year, many attached Tigers are suddenly quite content to sample the delights of cosy nights in with their beloveds. This could come as something of a culture shock for partners who are more used to solo suppers for one by the TV, or going out to drag Tiger back from their latest adventure. Yet, as long as the two of you still enjoy each other's company, 2023 could mark the beginning of a blissful new phase in your relationship.

Secrets of Success in 2023

Well, you're already a success, Tiger. If you're typical of your sign, you scored a record number of goals last year. The trouble is, you may not have seen the rewards of your efforts so far, so perhaps it doesn't feel as if you've done particularly well.

That's about to change in 2023. Recognition is coming your way, Tiger, and once it starts, it will snowball.

Your main challenge now is how you handle it. You can come over a bit abrupt at times, Tiger; you don't suffer fools, and you forget to hide your irritation. You don't really see why you should even try.

Well, that's not the Rabbit's way. The Rabbit encourages kind words, tactful behaviour, and politeness at all times, no matter how badly you're provoked.

If you can conduct yourself with grace, modesty, and patience, Tiger, the Rabbit will shower you with goodies.

Relapse into one of your snappy, irritable moods, or allow a sarcastic tone to creep into an exchange with an idiot, and you'll see some of your good fortune snatched away.

You've got some wonderful opportunities coming your way this year, Tiger – don't let them slip through your paws because of your own brusque manner.

The Tiger Year at a Glance

January – Even your stamina is flagging, Tiger. Yet you can sense brightness on the horizon.

February – This is more like it. You've recovered your bounce. Good news arrives from abroad.

March – A project stuck in a cul-de-sac suddenly frees itself. Now you're motoring.

April – A personality clash in the Tiger circle threatens. Back down, and think Rabbit. Diplomacy will bring surprising gains.

May – Jealousy looms around romance. Someone envies you. Be thankful you're an enviable person!

June – The boss or an important client thinks you're wonderful. A cash boost is coming your way.

July – Get ready for a career trip – possibly overseas. Recognition is yours. About time!

August – Looks like it's one trip after another. Work or leisure; suits you either way.

September – The Tiger love life looks up. Time for some exciting dates somewhere different.

October – A special offer, work-related, comes your way. A new role, a new career, more responsibility or maybe all three. Think carefully.

November – Foreign shores beckon, and it could be to do with your job. You may even relocate.

December – A family Christmas but not necessarily at yours. Children will bring joy to the festivities.

Lucky colours for 2023: Blue, White, Green

Lucky numbers for 2023: 3, 7

CHAPTER 14: BUT THEN THERE'S SO MUCH MORE TO YOU

So now you know your animal sign, but possibly you're thinking – okay, but how can everyone born in the same year as me have the same personality as me?

You've only got to think back to your class at school, full of children the same age as you, to know this can't be true. And you're absolutely right. What's more, Chinese astrologers agree with you. For this reason, in Chinese astrology, your birth year is only the beginning. The month you were born and the hour of your birth are also ruled by the twelve zodiac animals – and not necessarily the same animal that rules your birth year.

These other animals then go on to modify the qualities of your basic year personality. So someone born in an extrovert Tiger year but at the time of day ruled by the quieter Ox, and in the month of the softly spoken Snake, for instance, would very likely find their risk-taking Tiger qualities much toned down and enhanced by a few other calmer, more subtle traits.

By combining these three important influences, you get a much more accurate and detailed picture of the complex and unique person you really are. These calculations lead to so many permutations it soon becomes clear how people born in the same year can share various similarities, yet still remain quite different from each other.

What's more, the other animals linked to your date of birth can also have a bearing on how successful you will be in any year and how well you get on with people from other signs. Traditionally, the Horse and the Rabbit don't get on well together, for instance, so you'd expect two people born in these years to be unlikely to end up good friends. Yet if both individuals had other compatible signs in their charts, they could find themselves surprisingly warming to each other.

This is how it works:

Your Outer Animal – (Birth Year | Creates Your First Impression)

You're probably completely unaware of it, but when people meet you for the first time, they will sense the qualities represented by the animal that ruled your birth year. Your Outer Animal and its personality influence the way you appear to the outside world. Your Outer animal is your public face. You may not feel the least bit like this creature deep down, and you may wonder why nobody seems to understand the real you. Why is it that people always seem to underestimate you, or perhaps overestimate you, you may ask yourself frequently. The reason is that you just can't help giving the impression of your birth-year animal and people will tend to see you and think of you in this way – especially if they themselves were born in other years.

Your Inner Animal – (Birth Month | The Private You)

Your Inner Animal is the animal that rules the month in which you were born. The personality of this creature tells you a lot about how you feel inside, what motivates you, and how you tend to live your life. When you're out in the world and want to present yourself in the best light, it's easy for you to project the finest talents of your birth-year animal. You've got them at your fingertips. But at home, with no one you need to impress, your Inner Animal comes to the fore. You can kick back and relax. You may find you have abilities and interests that no one at work would ever guess. Only your closest friends and loved ones are likely to get to know your Inner Animal.

By now you know your Outer Animal so you can move on to find your Inner Animal from the chart below:

Month of Birth - Your Inner Animal

January – the Ox

February – the Tiger

March – the Rabbit

April – the Dragon

May – the Snake

June – the Horse

July – the Goat

August – the Monkey

September – the Rooster

October – the Dog

November – the Pig

December – the Rat

Your Secret Animal – (Birth Hour | The Still, Small Voice Within)

Your secret animal rules the time you were born. Each 24-hour period is divided into 12, two-hour time-slots and each slot is believed to be ruled by a particular animal. This animal represents the deepest, most secret part of you. It's possibly the most intimate, individual part of you as it marks the moment you first entered the world and became 'you'. This animal is possibly your conscience and your inspiration. It might represent qualities you'd like to have or sometimes fail to live up to. Chances are, no one else will ever meet your Secret Animal.

For your Secret Animal check out the time of your birth:

Hours of Birth – Your Secret Animal

1 am – 3 am – the Ox

3 am – 5 am – the Tiger

5 am – 7 am – the Rabbit

7 am – 9 am – the Dragon

9 am – 11 am – the Snake

11 am – 1.00 pm – the Horse

1.00 pm – 3.00 pm – the Goat

3.00 pm – 5.00 pm – the Monkey

5.00 pm – 7.00 pm – the Rooster

7.00 pm – 9.00 pm – the Dog

9.00 pm – 11.00 pm – the Pig

11.00 pm – 1.00 am – the Rat

When you've found your other animals, go back to the previous chapters and read the sections on those particular signs. You may well discover talents and traits that you recognise immediately as belonging to you in addition to those mentioned in your birth year. It could also be that your Inner Animal or your Secret Animal is the same as your Year animal. A Dragon born at 8 am in the morning, for instance, will be a secret Dragon inside as well as outside, because the hours between 7 am and 9 am are ruled by the Dragon.

When this happens, it suggests that the positive and the less positive attributes of the Dragon will be held in harmony, so this particular Dragon ends up being very well balanced.

You might also like to look at your new animal's compatibility with other signs and see where you might be able to widen your circle of friends and improve your love life.

CHAPTER 15: IN YOUR ELEMENT

There's no doubt about it, Chinese astrology has many layers. But then we all recognise that we have many facets to our personalities, too. We are all more complicated than we might first appear. And more unique, as well.

It turns out that even people who share the same Birth Year sign are not identical to people with the same sign but born in different years. A Rabbit born in 1963, for instance, will express their Rabbit personality in a slightly different way to a Rabbit born in 1975. This is not simply down to the influence of the other animals in their chart, it's because each year is also believed to be ruled by one of the five Chinese 'elements', as well as the year animal.

These elements are known as Water, Wood, Fire, Earth, and Metal.

Each element is thought to contain special qualities which are bestowed onto people born in the year it ruled, in addition to the qualities of their animal sign.

Since there are 12 signs endlessly rotating, and five elements, the same animal and element pairing only recurs once every 60 years. Which is why babies born in this 2023 Year of the Black Rabbit are unlikely to grow up remembering much about other Black Rabbits from the previous generation. Those senior Rabbits will already be 60-years-old when the baby bunnies are born.

In years gone by, when life expectancy was much lower, the chances are there would only ever be one generation of a particular combined sign and element alive in the world at a time.

Find Your Element from the Chart Below:

The 1920s

5 February 1924 – 24 January 1925 | RAT | WOOD

25 January 1925 – 12 February 1926 | OX | WOOD

13 February 1926 – 1 February 1927 | TIGER | FIRE

2 February 1927 – 22 January 1928 | RABBIT | FIRE

23 January 1928 – 9 February 1929 | DRAGON | EARTH

10 February 1929 – 29 January 1930 | SNAKE | EARTH

The 1930s

30 January 1930 – 16 February 1931 | HORSE | METAL

17 February 1931 – 5 February 1932 | GOAT | METAL

6 February 1932 – 25 January 1933 | MONKEY | WATER

26 January 1933 – 13 February 1934 | ROOSTER | WATER

14 February 1934 – 3 February 1935 | DOG | WOOD

4 February 1935 – 23 January 1936 | PIG | WOOD

24 January 1936 – 10 February 1937 | RAT | FIRE

11 February 1937 – 30 January 1938 | OX | FIRE

31 January 1938 – 18 February 1939 | TIGER | EARTH

19 February 1939 – 7 February 1940 | RABBIT | EARTH

The 1940s

8 February 1940 – 26 January 1941 | DRAGON | METAL

27 January 1941 – 14 February 1942 | SNAKE | METAL

15 February 1942 – 4 February 1943 | HORSE | WATER

5 February 1943 – 24 January 1944 | GOAT | WATER

25 January 1944 – 12 February 1945 | MONKEY | WOOD

13 February 1945 – 1 February 1946 | ROOSTER | WOOD

2 February 1946 – 21 January 1947 | DOG | FIRE

22 January 1947 – 9 February 1948 | PIG | FIRE

10 February 1948 – 28 January 1949 | RAT | EARTH

29 January 1949 – 16 February 1950 | OX | EARTH

The 1950s

17 February 1950 – 5 February 1951 | TIGER | METAL

6 February 1951 – 26 January 1952 | RABBIT | METAL

27 January 1952 – 13 February 1953 | DRAGON | WATER

14 February 1953 – 2 February 1954 | SNAKE | WATER

3 February 1954 – 23 January 1955 | HORSE | WOOD

24 January 1955 – 11 February 1956 | GOAT | WOOD

12 February 1956 – 30 January 1957 | MONKEY | FIRE

31 January 1957 – 17 February 1958 | ROOSTER | FIRE

18 February 1958 – 7 February 1959 | DOG | EARTH

8 February 1959 – 27 January 1960 | PIG | EARTH

The 1960s

28 January 1960 – 14 February 1961 | RAT | METAL

15 February 1961 – 4 February 1962 | OX | METAL

5 February 1962 – 24 January 1963 | TIGER | WATER

25 January 1963 – 12 February 1964 | RABBIT | WATER

13 February 1964 – 1 February 1965 | DRAGON | WOOD

2 February 1965 – 20 January 1966 | SNAKE | WOOD

21 January 1966 – 8 February 1967 | HORSE | FIRE

9 February 1967 – 29 January 1968 | GOAT | FIRE

30 January 1968 – 16 February 1969 | MONKEY | EARTH

17 February 1969 – 5 February 1970 | ROOSTER | EARTH

The 1970s

6 February 1970 – 26 January 1971 | DOG | METAL

27 January 1971 – 14 February 1972 | PIG | METAL

15 February 1972 – 2 February 1973 | RAT | WATER

3 February 1973 – 22 January 1974 | OX | WATER

23 January 1974 – 10 February 1975 | TIGER | WOOD

11 February 1975 – 30 January 1976 | RABBIT | WOOD

31 January 1976 – 17 February 1977 | DRAGON | FIRE

18 February 1977 – 6 February 1978 | SNAKE | FIRE

7 February 1978 – 27 January 1979 | HORSE | EARTH

28 January 1979 – 15 February 1980 | GOAT | EARTH

The 1980s

16 February 1980 – 4 February 1981 | MONKEY | METAL

5 February 1981 – 24 January 1982 | ROOSTER | METAL

25 January 1982 – 12 February 1983 | DOG | WATER

13 February 1983 – 1 February 1984 | PIG | WATER

2 February 1984 – 19 February 1985 | RAT | WOOD

20 February 1985 – 8 February 1986 | OX | WOOD

9 February 1986 – 28 January 1987 | TIGER | FIRE

29 January 1987 – 16 February 1988 | RABBIT | FIRE

17 February 1988 – 5 February 1989 | DRAGON | EARTH

6 February 1989 – 26 January 1990 | SNAKE | EARTH

The 1990s

27 January 1990 – 14 February 1991 | HORSE | METAL

15 February 1991 – 3 February 1992 | GOAT | METAL

4 February 1992 – 22 January 1993 | MONKEY | WATER

23 January 1993 – 9 February 1994 | ROOSTER | WATER

10 February 1994 – 30 January 1995 | DOG | WOOD

31 January 1995 – 18 February 1996 | PIG | WOOD

19 February 1996 – 7 February 1997 | RAT | FIRE

8 February 1997 – 27 January 1998 | OX | FIRE

28 January 1998 – 5 February 1999 | TIGER | EARTH

6 February 1999 – 4 February 2000 | RABBIT | EARTH

The 2000s

5 February 2000 – 23 January 2001 | DRAGON | METAL

24 January 2001 – 11 February 2002 | SNAKE | METAL

12 February 2002 – 31 January 2003 | HORSE | WATER

1 February 2003 – 21 January 2004 | GOAT | WATER

22 January 2004 – 8 February 2005 | MONKEY | WOOD

9 February 2005 – 28 January 2006 | ROOSTER | WOOD

29 January 2006 – 17 February 2007 | DOG | FIRE

18 February 2007 – 6 February 2008 | PIG | FIRE

7 February 2008 – 25 January 2009 | RAT | EARTH

26 January 2009 – 13 February 2010 | OX | EARTH

The 2010s

14 February 2010 – 2 February 2011 | TIGER | METAL

3 February 2011 – 22 January 2012 | RABBIT | METAL

23 January 2012 – 9 February 2013 | DRAGON | WATER

10 February 2013 – 30 January 2014 | SNAKE | WATER

31 January 2014 – 18 February 2015 | HORSE | WOOD

19 February 2015 – 7 February 2016 | GOAT | WOOD

8 February 2016 – 27 January 2017 | MONKEY | FIRE

28 January 2017 – 15 February 2018 | ROOSTER | FIRE

16 February 2018 – 4 February 2019 | DOG | EARTH

5 February 2019 – 24 January 2020 | PIG | EARTH

The 2020s

25 January 2020 – 11 February 2021 | RAT | METAL

12 February 2021 – 1 February 2022 | OX | METAL

2 February 2022 – 21 January 2023 | TIGER | WATER

22 January 2023 – 9 February 2024 | RABBIT | WATER

10 February 2024 – 28 January 2025 | DRAGON | WOOD

29 January 2025 – 16 February 2026 | SNAKE | WOOD

17 February 2026 – 5 February 2027 | HORSE | FIRE

6 February 2027 – 25 January 2028 | GOAT | FIRE

26 January 2028 – 12 February 2029 | MONKEY | EARTH

13 February 2029 – 2 February 2030 | ROOSTER | EARTH

You may have noticed that the 'natural' basic element of your sign is not necessarily the same as the element of the year you were born. Don't worry about this. The element of your birth year takes precedence, though you could also read the qualities assigned to the natural element as well, as these will be relevant to your personality but to a lesser degree.

Metal

Metal is the element associated in China with gold and wealth. So if you are a Metal child, you will be very good at accumulating money. The Metal individual is ambitious, even if their animal sign is not particularly career-minded. The Metal-born version of an unworldly sign will still somehow have an eye for a bargain or a good investment; they'll manage to buy at the right time when prices are low and be moved to sell just as the price is peaking. If they want to get rid of unwanted items, they'll potter along to a car boot sale and without appearing to try, somehow make a killing, selling the lot while stalls around them struggle for attention. Career-minded signs with the element Metal have to be careful they don't overdo things. They have a tendency to become workaholics. Wealth will certainly flow, but it could be at the expense of family harmony and social life.

The element of Metal adds power, drive, and tenacity to whatever sign it influences so if you were born in a Metal year you'll never lack cash for long.

Water

Water is the element associated with communication, creativity, and the emotions. Water has a knack of flowing around obstacles, finding routes that are not obvious to the naked eye and seeping into the smallest cracks. So if you're a Water child, you'll be very good at getting what you want in an oblique, unchallenging way. You are one of nature's lateral thinkers. You are also wonderful with people. You're sympathetic, empathetic, and can always find the right words at the right time. You can also be highly persuasive, but in such a subtle way nobody notices your influence or input. They think the whole thing was their own idea.

People born in Water years are very creative and extremely intuitive. They don't know where their inspiration comes from, but somehow ideas just pour into their brains. Many artists were born in Water years.

Animal signs that are normally regarded as a little impatient and tactless have their rough edges smoothed when they appear in a Water year. People born in these years will be more diplomatic, artistic, and amiable than other versions of their fellow signs. And if you were born in a naturally sensitive, emotional sign, in a Water year, you'll be so intuitive you're probably psychic. Yet just as water can fall as gentle nurturing rain, or a raging destructive flood, so Water types need to take care not to let their emotions run away with them or to allow themselves to use their persuasive skills to be too manipulative.

Wood

Wood is the element associated with growth and expansion. In Chinese astrology, Wood doesn't primarily refer to the inert variety used to make floorboards and furniture, it represents living, flourishing trees and smaller plants, all pushing out of the earth and growing towards the sky.

Wood is represented by the colour green, not brown. If you're a Wood child, you're likely to be honest, generous, and friendly. You think BIG and like to be involved in numerous projects, often at the same time.

Wood people are practical yet imaginative and able to enlist the support of others simply by the sincerity and enthusiasm with which they tackle their plans. Yet even though they're always busy with a project, they somehow radiate calm, stability, and confidence. There's a sense of the timeless serenity of a big old tree about Wood people. Other signs instinctively trust them and look to them for guidance.

Animal signs that could be prone to nervousness or impulsive behaviour tend to be calmer and more productive in Wood year versions, while signs whose natural element is also Wood could well end up leaders of vast teams or business empires. Wood people tend to sail smoothly through life, but they must guard against becoming either stubborn or unyielding as they grow older or alternatively, saying 'yes' to every new plan and overextending themselves.

Fire

Fire is the element associated with dynamism, strength, and persistence. Fire demands action, movement, and expansion. It also creates a huge amount of heat. Fire is precious when it warms our homes and cooks our food, and it possesses a savage beauty that's endlessly fascinating. Yet it's also highly dangerous and destructive if it gets out of control. Something of this ambivalent quality is evident in Fire children.

People born in Fire years tend to be immensely attractive, magnetic types. Other signs are drawn to them. Yet there is always a hint of danger, of unpredictability, about them. You never know quite where you are with a Fire year sign and in a way, this is part of their fascination.

People born in Fire years like to get things done. They are extroverted and bold and impatient for action. They are brilliant at getting things started and energising people and projects. Quieter signs born in a Fire year are more dynamic, outspoken, and energetic than their fellow sign cousins, while extrovert signs positively blaze with exuberance and confidence when Fire is added to the mix.

People born in Fire years will always be noticed, but they should try to remember they tend to be impatient and impulsive. Develop a habit of pausing to take a deep breath to consider things, before rushing in, and you won't get burned.

Earth

Earth is the element associated with patience, stability, and practicality. This may not sound exciting but, in Chinese astrology, Earth is at the centre of everything: the heart of the planet. Earth year children are strong, hardworking personalities. They will persist with a task if it's worthwhile and never give up until it's complete. They create structure and balance, and they have very nurturing instincts.

Women born in Earth years make wonderful mothers, and if they're not mothering actual children, they'll be mothering their colleagues at work, or their friends and relatives, while also filling their homes with houseplants and raising vegetables in the garden if at all possible.

Other signs like being around Earth types as they exude a sense of security. Earth people don't like change, and they strive to keep their lives settled and harmonious. They are deeply kind and caring and immensely honest. Tact is not one of their strong points, however. They will always say what they think, so if you don't want the unvarnished truth, better not to ask!

Earth lends patience and stability to the more flighty, over-emotional signs, and rock solid integrity to the others. Earth people will be sought-after in whatever field they choose to enter, but they must take care not to become too stubborn. Make a point of seeking out and listening to a wide range of varying opinions before setting a decision in stone.

Yin and Yang

As you looked down the table of years and elements, you may have noticed that the elements came in pairs. Each element was repeated the following year. If the Monkey was Water one year, it would be followed immediately the next year by the Rooster, also Water.

This is because of Yin and Yang – the mysterious but vital forces that, in Chinese philosophy, are believed to control the planet and probably the whole universe. They can be thought of as positive and negative, light and dark, masculine and feminine, night and day, etc. but the important point is that everything is either Yin or Yang; the two forces complement each other and both are equally important because only together do they make up the whole. For peace and harmony to be achieved, both forces need to be in balance.

Each of the animal signs is believed to be either Yin or Yang and because of the need for balance and harmony, they alternate through the years. Six of the 12 signs are Yin and six are Yang and since Yang represents extrovert, dominant energy, the Yang sign is first, followed by the Yin sign which represents quiet, passive force. A Yang sign is always followed by a Yin sign throughout the cycle.

The Yang signs are:

Rat

Tiger

Dragon

Horse

Monkey

Dog

The Yin Signs are

Ox

Rabbit

Snake

Goat

Rooster

Pig

Although Yang is seen as a masculine energy, and Yin a feminine energy, in reality, whether you are male or female, everyone has a mixture of Yin and Yang within them. If you need to know, quickly, whether your sign is Yin or Yang just check your birth year. If it ends in an even number (or 0) your sign is Yang. If it ends in an odd number, your sign is Yin. (The only exception is if you're born in late January or early February and according to Chinese astrology you belong to the year before).

In general, Yang signs tend to be extrovert, action-oriented types while Yin signs are gentler, more thoughtful, and patient.

So, as balance is essential when an element controls a period of time, it needs to express itself in its stronger Yang form in a Yang year as well as in its gentler Yin form in a Yin year, to be complete.

This year of the Black Water Rabbit completes the round of the Water element. Last year it was in its Yang form accompanied by the Tiger, now it draws to a close in its Yin form with the Water Rabbit.

Next year the Wood element will begin and Water will not come round again until 2032.

But why do elements have two forms? It's to take into account the great variations in strength encompassed by an element. The difference between a candle flame and a raging inferno – both belonging to Fire; or a great oak tree and a blade of grass – both belonging to the Wood element. Each has to get the chance to be expressed to create balance.

So, in Yang years, the influence of the ruling element will be particularly strong. In Yin years, the same element expresses itself in its gentler form.

Friendly Elements

Just as some signs get on well together and others don't, so some elements work well together while others don't. These are the elements that exist in harmony:

METAL likes EARTH and WATER

WATER likes METAL and WOOD

WOOD likes WATER and FIRE

FIRE likes WOOD and EARTH

EARTH likes FIRE and METAL

The reason for these friendly partnerships is believed to be the natural, productive cycle. Water nourishes Wood and makes plants grow, Wood provides fuel for Fire, Fire produces ash which is a type of Earth, Earth can be melted or mined to produce Metal while Metal contains or carries Water in a bucket.

So, Water supports Wood, Wood supports Fire, Fire supports Earth, Earth supports Metal and Metal supports Water.

Unfriendly Elements

But since everything has to be in balance, all the friendly elements are opposed by the same number of unfriendly elements. These are the elements that are not in harmony:

METAL dislikes WOOD and FIRE

WATER dislikes FIRE and EARTH

WOOD dislikes EARTH and METAL

FIRE dislikes METAL and WATER

EARTH dislikes WOOD and WATER

The reason some elements don't get on is down to the destructive cycle which is: Water puts out Fire and is absorbed by Earth, Wood breaks up Earth (with its strong roots) and is harmed by Metal tools, Metal is melted by Fire and can cut down Wood.

So if someone just seems to rub you up the wrong way, for no logical reason, it could be that your elements clash.

CHAPTER 16: WESTERN HOROSCOPES AND CHINESE HOROSCOPES – THE LINK

So now, hopefully, you'll have all the tools you need to create your very own, personal, multi-faceted Chinese horoscope. But does that mean the Western-style astrological sign that you're more familiar with is no longer relevant?

Not necessarily. Purists may not agree, but the odd thing is there does seem to be an overlap between a person's Western birth sign and their Chinese birth month sign; the two together can add yet another interesting layer to the basic birth year personality.

A Rabbit born under the Western sign of Leo may turn out to be very different on the surface, to a Rabbit born under the Western sign of Pisces for instance.

Of course, Chinese astrology already takes this into account by including the season of birth in a full chart, but we can possibly refine the system even further by adding the characteristics we've learned from our Western Sun Signs into the jigsaw.

If you'd like to put this theory to the test, simply find your Chinese year sign and then look up your Western Astrological sign within it, from the list below. While you're at it, why not check out the readings for your partner and friends too? You could be amazed at how accurate the results turn out to be.

Rabbit

Aries Rabbit

This is a very dynamic Rabbit. When powerful Aries injects a streak of energy into that cultured Rabbit personality, the result is a wonderfully clever individual who glides effortlessly to success. Although at times Aries Rabbit has an attack of over-cautiousness, these types are usually bolder than the average bunny and achieve much where other Rabbits might run away. Occasionally, these Rabbits will even take a gamble, and this is worthwhile as it usually pays off for them.

Taurus Rabbit

The Taurus Rabbit really does feel his home is his castle. He is not unduly interested in his career, but he is likely to turn his home into an art form. Brilliant entertainers, these types guarantee their lucky guests will enjoy all the creature comforts possible. They often marry later in life than average, but when they do, they work at the relationship. Providing they choose another home bird, they are likely to be very happy.

Gemini Rabbit

All Rabbits are natural diplomats, but the Gemini Rabbit really is the star of them all. So skilled a communicator is this creature, so expert at people management that a career in the diplomatic service, politics, psychology or even advertising is an option. Never lost for words, these types can persuade anyone to do almost anything. As a result, they are usually very successful. Once they harness their enviable skills to a worthwhile career, they can go far.

Cancer Rabbit

Cancer Rabbits are gentle, kindly souls. They like to be surrounded by pleasant company and prefer to have few demands put upon them. They don't really take to business life and find many professions too abrasive.

On the other hand, they find working for themselves too stressful a venture to be considered seriously. They are happiest in a peaceful, routine environment where they can make steady progress, but really their hearts are at home. Home is where they express themselves.

Leo Rabbit

Leo Rabbits, on the other hand, are usually very popular with a wide circle of friends. Extrovert Leo gives Rabbit a strong dose of confidence and flair, and when these qualities are added to Rabbit's people skills, a radiant, magnetic individual is born. Leo Rabbits adore parties where they shine. They are always elegant and beautifully turned out and have a knack of putting others at their ease. These Rabbits climb the ladder of success very quickly.

Virgo Rabbit

Virgo Rabbits have a lot on their minds. The natural cautiousness of the Rabbit is heightened by the same quality in Virgo, and these Rabbits tend to be born worriers. They are masters of detail but, unfortunately, this often leads them to make mountains out of molehills. They are very talented creatures but too often fail to make the best use of their gifts because they spend so much time worrying about all the things that could go wrong. If they can learn to relax and take the odd risk now and then, they will go far.

Libra Rabbit

Art-loving Libra blends easily into the cultured sign of the Rabbit. These types love to learn more about beautiful things, and they like to share their knowledge with others. They are so good with people that they can convey information effortlessly and make the dullest subject sound interesting. These types are often gifted teachers and lecturers though they would find difficult inner-city schools too traumatic. Give these types willing and interested pupils, and they blossom.

Scorpio Rabbit

Rabbits tend to be discreet people, and Scorpio Rabbits are the most tight-lipped of the lot. Scorpio Rabbits have a lot of secrets, and they enjoy keeping them. It gives them a wonderful feeling of superiority to think that they know things others don't. They have many secret ambitions too, and they don't like to speak of them in case others are pessimistic and pour scorn on their plans. So it is the Scorpio Rabbit who is most likely to surprise everyone by suddenly reaching an amazing goal that no-one even knew he was aiming for.

Sagittarius Rabbit

Sporty Sagittarius brings a whole new dimension to the art-loving Rabbit. Rabbits are often indoor creatures, but Sagittarian Rabbits are much more adventurous in the open air than the usual bunny. They are sensuous and fun and attract many friends. They are also versatile and can turn their hands to several different careers if necessary. They like to get out and about more than most Rabbits and they are usually very successful.

Capricorn Rabbit

Capricorn Rabbits are great family folk. They firmly believe the family is the bedrock of life, and they work hard to keep their relations happy and together. The Capricorn Rabbit home is the centre of numerous clan gatherings throughout the year and weddings, birthdays, anniversaries and christenings are very important to them. Capricorn Rabbit will never forget the dates. These types are particularly interested in the past and will enjoy researching a family tree going back generations. If it ever crosses their minds that the rest of the tribe seems to leave all the donkey work to Capricorn Rabbit, he'd never say so. And, in truth, he doesn't really mind. There's nothing he loves more than having his family around him.

Aquarius Rabbit

The Aquarius Rabbit is a contradictory creature being both cautious and curious at the same time. These types crave security and love, and yet they have a great longing to find out more about everything around them. Fascinated by art, science and new inventions they love to potter about in book shops and tinker in the shed at home. Once they get an idea in their head, they can't rest until they have experimented with it, frequently forgetting to eat while they work. They need love and understanding.

Pisces Rabbit

The Pisces Rabbit is another bunny who needs a lot of understanding. Often gifted artistically they can sometimes be stubborn and awkward for no apparent reason. Yet when they are in the right frame of mind, they can charm the birds off the trees. It takes them a long time to make a friend, but when they do, it is a friend for life. The Pisces Rabbit home is full of beautiful things, and these subjects love to invite their most trusted friends to come and enjoy the magic.

Dragon

Aries Dragon

The Dragon is already a powerful sign, but when the lively influence of Aries is added, you have a positively devastating individual. These are the types that others either love or loathe. Strong, confident people can cope happily with the Aries Dragon, but more timid souls are terrified. The Aries Dragon himself is quite unaware of the reaction he causes. He goes busily on his way oblivious of the earthquakes all around him. These types have to guard against arrogance, particularly since they have quite a lot to be arrogant about. They also have a tendency to get bored easily and move on to new projects without completing the old, which is a pity since they can accomplish much if they persevere.

Taurus Dragon

There is something magnificent about the Taurus Dragon. Large, expansive types, they move easily around the social scene spreading bonhomie wherever they go. Not the most sensitive of individuals, they find it difficult to assess the moods of others and assume everyone else feels the same way they do. Should it be brought to their attention that someone is unhappy, however, they will move heaven and earth to cheer them up. These types are reliable and conscientious and always keep their promises.

Gemini Dragon

Dragons may not have the quickest minds in the Chinese zodiac, but Gemini Dragons are speedier than most. They are jovial types with a brilliant sense of humour. In fact, they can cleverly joke others into doing what they want. These types have no need for physical force to get their own way; they use laughter instead. At times, Gemini Dragons can be almost devious, which is unusual for a Dragon but nobody really minds their schemes. They give everyone such a good time on the way it's worth doing what they want for the sheer entertainment.

Cancer Dragon

Cautious Cancer and flamboyant Dragon make a surprisingly good combination. Cancer holds Dragon back where he might go too far, while Dragon endows the Crab with exuberance and style. These types like to help others make the most of themselves, but they are also high achievers in their own right. Without upsetting anyone, Cancer Dragons tend to zoom to the top faster than most.

Leo Dragon

This Dragon is so dazzling you need sunglasses to look at him. The proud, glorious Lion combined with the magnificent Dragon is an extraordinary combination, and it's fortunate it only comes around once every twelve years. Too many of such splendid creatures would be hard to take. Leo Dragons really do have star quality, and they know it. They demand to be the centre of attention and praise is like oxygen to them – they can't live without it. Yet they have generous hearts, and if anyone is in trouble, Leo Dragon will be the first to rush to their assistance.

Virgo Dragon

Unusually for a Dragon, the Virgo variety can get quite aggressive if crossed, but this doesn't often happen as very few people would dare take on such a daunting beast. These types are immensely clever in business. They steadily add acquisition to shrewd acquisition until they end up seriously rich. They are wilier than most Dragons who have a surprisingly naive streak, and they make the most of it. These types just can't help becoming successful in whatever they undertake.

Libra Dragon

Dragons are not usually too bothered about trifles such as fine clothes and wallpaper. In fact, some older, more absent-minded Dragons have been known to go shopping in their slippers having forgotten to take them off. The exception is the Dragon born under the sign of Libra. These types are more down to earth and see the sense in putting on a good show for others. They take the trouble to choose smart clothes and keep them looking that way at all times. They are also more intuitive and are not easily fooled by others.

Scorpio Dragon

Handling money is not a Dragon strong point, but the Scorpio variety has more ability in this direction than most. Scorpio Dragons enjoy amassing cash. Rather like their legendary namesakes who hoard treasure in their lairs, Scorpio Dragons like to build substantial nest-eggs and keep them close at hand where they can admire them regularly. These types can also be a little stingy financially, not out of true meanness but simply because they don't like to see their carefully guarded heap diminish in size. Once they understand the importance of a purchase, however, they can be just as generous as their brothers and sisters.

Sagittarius Dragon

When Sagittarius joins the Dragon, the combination produces a real livewire, a true daredevil. The antics of the Sagittarius Dragon, when young, will give their mothers nightmares and later drive their partners to drink. These types can't resist a challenge, particularly a dangerous one. They will climb mountain peaks, leap off cliffs on a hang-glider and try a spot of bungee-jumping to enliven a dull moment. It's no good expecting these types to sit down with a good book; they just can't keep still. However, surrounded by friends, dashing from one perilous venture to the next, the Sagittarius Dragon is one of the happiest people around.

Capricorn Dragon

The Capricorn Dragon looks back at his Sagittarian brother in horror. He simply can't understand the need for such pranks. Being Dragons, these types are bold, but the influence of Capricorn ensures that they are never foolhardy. They look before they leap and occasionally miss a good deal because they stop to check the fine print. They are not the most intuitive of creatures, but show them a needy soul and they will efficiently do whatever's necessary to help. The Capricorn Dragon is a highly effective creature.

Aquarius Dragon

Happy go lucky types, the Aquarius Dragons are usually surrounded by people. Honest and hardworking, they will put in just as much effort for very little cash as they will for a great deal. If someone asks them to do a job and they agree to do it, they will move heaven and earth to fulfil their obligations even if it is not in their best interests to do so. However, they're not suited to routine, and if a task doesn't interest them, they will avoid it at all costs no matter how well paid it might be. Not particularly interested in money for its own sake, these types are sociable and easy to get along with. They are often highly talented in some way.

Pisces Dragon

Pisces Dragons, on the other hand, are surprisingly good with cash. Despite their often vague, good-humoured exteriors these types have excellent financial brains and seem to know just what to do to increase their savings. They are first in the queue when bargains are to be found, and they seem to sense what the next money-making trend is going to be before anyone else has thought of it. These types often end up quite wealthy and excel, particularly, in artistic fields.

Snake

Aries Snake

Generally speaking, Snakes tend to lack energy, so the influence of dynamic Aries is very welcome indeed. These subjects are highly intelligent, well-motivated and never leave anything unfinished. They are achievers and will not give up until they reach their goal – which they invariably do. Nothing can stand in the way of Aries Snakes, and they reach the top of whatever tree they climb.

Taurus Snake

In contrast, the sensuous Taurus Snake really can't be bothered with all that hard work. Taurus Snakes have great ability, but they will only do as much as is necessary to acquire the lifestyle they desire, and then they like to sit back and enjoy it. Tremendous sun worshippers, the Taurus Snakes would be quite happy to be on a permanent holiday, providing the accommodation was a five-star hotel with a fabulous restaurant.

Gemini Snake

The Gemini Snake can be a slippery customer. A brilliant brain, linked to a shrewd but amusing tongue, these types can run rings around almost everybody. They can scheme and manipulate if it suits them and pull off all sorts of audacious tricks but having achieved much, they tend to get bored and lose interest, giving up on the brink of great things. This often leads to conflict with business associates who cannot understand such contradictory behaviour. Insane they call it. Suicidal. The Gemini Snake just shrugs and moves on.

Cancer Snake

The Snake born under the sign of Cancer is a more conventional creature. These types will at least do all that is required of them and bring their formidable Snake brains to bear on the task in hand. They are gifted researchers, historians and archaeologists – any career which involves deep concentration and patient study. But the Cancer Snake must take care to mix with cheerful people since left to himself he has a tendency for melancholy. Warmth, laughter, and plenty of rest transforms the Cancer Snake and allows those unique talents to blossom.

Leo Snake

The Leo Snake is a very seductive creature. Beautifully dressed, sparklingly magnetic, few people can take their eyes off these types, and they know it. All Snakes are sensuous, but the Snake born under the sign of Leo is probably the most sensuous of the lot. Never short of admirers, these types are not eager to settle down. Why should they when they're having such a good time? Late in life, the Leo Snake may consent to get married if their partner can offer them a good enough life. If not, these types are quite content to go it alone – probably because they are never truly on their own. They collect willing followers right into old age.

Virgo Snake

The Virgo Snake is another fascinating combination. Highly intuitive and wildly passionate, the Virgo Snake is all elegant understatement on the outside and erotic abandon on the inside. The opposite sex is mesmerised by this intriguing contradiction and just can't stay away. Virgo Snakes can achieve success in their careers if they put their minds to it, but often they are having too much fun flirting and flitting from one lover to the next. Faithfulness is not their strong point, but they are so sexy they get away with murder.

Libra Snake

When you see a top model slinking sinuously down the catwalk, she could very well be a Libra Snake. Snakes born under this sign are the most elegant and stylish of the lot. They may not be conventionally good looking, but they will turn heads wherever they go. These types really understand clothes and could make a plastic bin-liner look glamorous just by putting it on. Somehow they have the knack of stepping off a transatlantic flight without a crease and driving an open-topped sports car without ruffling their hair. No-one knows quite how they achieve these feats, and Libra Snake isn't telling.

Scorpio Snake

The Snake born under Scorpio is destined to have a complicated life. These types enjoy plots and intrigues, particularly of a romantic nature and spend endless hours devising schemes and planning subterfuge. That ingenious Snake brain is capable of brewing up the most elaborate scams, and there's nothing Scorpio Snake loves more than watching all the parts fall into place. But schemes have a knack of going wrong, and schemers have to change their plans and change them again to cope with each new contingency as it arises. If he's not careful, the Scorpio Snake can become hopelessly embroiled in his own plot.

Sagittarius Snake

Traditionally other signs are wary of the Snake and tend to hold back a little from them without knowing why. When the Snake is born under Sagittarius, however, the subject seems more approachable than most.

Sagittarian Snakes sooner or later become recognised for their wisdom and down to earth good sense and people flock to them for advice. Without ever intending to, the Sagittarius Snake could end up as something of a guru attracting eager acolytes desperate to learn more.

Capricorn Snake

The Snake born under Capricorn is more ambitious than the average serpent. These types will reach for the stars and grasp them. Obstacles just melt away when faced with the dual-beam of Capricorn Snake intelligence and quiet persistence. These Snakes are good providers and more dependable than most Snakes. They often end up surrounded by all the trappings of success, but they accomplish this so quietly, no one can quite work out how they managed it.

Aquarius Snake

Another highly intuitive Snake. Independent but people-loving Aquarius endows the serpent with greater social skills than usual. These types attract many friends, and they have the ability to understand just how others are feeling without them having to say a word. These Snakes have particularly enquiring minds, and they can't pass a museum or book shop without going in to browse. Born researchers, they love to dig and delve into whatever subject has taken their fancy, no matter how obscure. Quite often, they discover something valuable by accident.

Pisces Snake

Pisces Snakes tend to live on their nerves even more than most. These types are friendly up to a point, but they hate disagreements and problems and withdraw when things look unpleasant. They are sexy and sensuous and would much prefer a quiet evening with just one special person than a wild party. In the privacy of their bedroom, anything goes, and Pisces Snakes reveal the naughty side of their characters. No one would guess from the understated elegance of their exteriors what an erotic creature the Pisces Snake really is.

Horse

Aries Horse

Overflowing with energy the Aries Horse just can't sit still for long. These types just have to find an outlet for their phenomenal vitality. They are hardworking, hard-playing, and usually highly popular. Less fun-loving signs might be accused of being workaholics but not the Aries Horse. People born under this sign devote enormous amounts of time to their careers but still have so much spare capacity there is plenty left over for their friends. They always do well in their chosen profession.

Taurus Horse

The Taurus Horse can be a trickier creature. Charming yet logical, he has a very good brain and is not afraid to use it. The only problem is that without warning the Taurus Horse can turn from flighty and fun to immensely stubborn and even an earthquake wouldn't shift him from an entrenched position. Yet treated with understanding and patience, the Taurus Horse can be coaxed to produce wonderful achievements.

Gemini Horse

Gemini types are easily bored, and when they are born in the freedom-loving year of the Horse, this trait tends to be accentuated. Unless their attention is caught and held almost instantly, Gemini Horse subjects kick up their heels and gallop off to find more fun elsewhere. For this reason, they often find it difficult to hold on to a job, and they change careers frequently. Yet once they discover a subject about which they can feel passionate, they employ the whole of their considerable talent and will zoom to the top in record time.

Cancer Horse

The Cancer Horse is a lovable creature with a great many friends. These types tend to lack confidence and need a lot of praise and nurturing, but with the right leadership, they will move mountains. Some signs find them difficult to understand because the Cancer Horse loves to be surrounded by a crowd yet needs a lot of alone time too. Misjudge the mood, and the Cancer Horse can seem bafflingly unfriendly. Yet, stay the course, and these subjects become wonderfully loyal friends.

Leo Horse

People born under the star sign of Leo will be the first to admit they like to show off and when they are also born in the year of the Horse, they enjoy showing off all the more. These types love nothing better than strutting around rocking designer outfits while others look on in admiration. They are not so interested in home decor; it's their own personal appearance which counts most. The Leo Horse would much rather invest time and money boosting their image than shoving their earnings into a bank account to gather dust.

Virgo Horse

Virgo types can be a little solemn and over-devoted to duty, but when they are born in the year of the Horse, they are endowed with a welcome streak of equine frivolity. The Virgo Horse loves to party. He will make sure his work is completed first of course, but once the office door clicks shut behind him, the Virgo Horse really knows how to let his hair down.

Libra Horse

The Libra Horse is another true charmer. Friends and acquaintances by the score fill the address books of these types, and their diaries are crammed with appointments. Honest, trustworthy and helpful, other people can't help gravitating to them. Oddly enough, despite their gregarious nature, these types are also very independent. Sometimes too independent for their own good. They are excellent at giving advice to others but find it almost impossible to take advice themselves.

Scorpio Horse

The Scorpio Horse is a real thrill seeker. These types enjoy life's pleasures, particularly passionate pleasures and go all out to attain them. There is no middle road with the Scorpio Horse. These are all or nothing types. They fling themselves into the project of the moment wholeheartedly or not at all. They tend to see things in black and white and believe others are either for them or against them. In serious moments, the Scorpio Horse subscribes to some surprising conspiracy theories, but mostly they keep these ideas to themselves.

Sagittarius Horse

The star sign of Sagittarius is the sign of the Centaur – half-man half-horse – and when these types are born in the year of the Horse, the equine tendencies are so strong they practically have four hooves. Carefree country-lovers these subjects can't bear to be penned in and never feel totally happy until they are out of doors in some wide-open space. They crave fresh air and regular exercise and do best in joint activities. As long as they can spend enough time out of doors, Sagittarius Horses are blessed with glowing good health.

Capricorn Horse

The Capricorn Horse is a canny beast. These types are great savers. They manage to have fun on a shoestring and stash away every spare penny at the same time. They are prepared to work immensely hard provided the pay is good, and they have a remarkable knack of finding just the right job to make the most of their earning power. The Capricorn Horse likes a good time, and he will never be poor.

Aquarius Horse

When Aquarius meets the Horse, it results in a very curious creature. These types admit to enquiring minds; other less charitable signs might call them nosey parkers. Call them what you may, subjects born under this sign need to know and discover. They often become inventors, and they have a weakness for new gadgets and the latest technology. The Aquarius Horse can be wildly impractical and annoy partners by frittering cash away on their latest obsession. They also tend to fill their living space with peculiar objects from junk shops and car boot sales, which they intend to upcycle into useful treasures. Somehow, they seldom get round to finishing the project.

Pisces Horse

Artistic Pisces adds an unusual dimension to the physical Horse, who normally has little time for cultural frills and foibles. These types are great home entertainers and often gifted cooks as well. They invite a group of friends around at the slightest excuse and can conjure delicious snacks and drinks from the most unpromising larders. They adore company and get melancholy if left alone too long.

Goat

Aries Goat

Normally mild and unassuming, the Goat can become almost argumentative when born under the star sign of Aries. Though friendly and very seldom cross, the Aries Goat will suddenly adopt an unexpectedly stubborn position and stick to it unreasonably even when it's obvious he is wrong. Despite this, these types are blessed with sunny natures and are quickly forgiven. They don't bear a grudge and have no idea – after the awkwardness – that anything unpleasant occurred.

Taurus Goat

Like his Aries cousin, the Taurus Goat can turn stubborn too. These types have a very long fuse. Most people would assume they did not have a temper because it is so rarely displayed. But make them truly angry, and they will explode. Small they may be, but a raging Goat can be a fearful sight. On the other hand, these Goats are more likely to have a sweet tooth than their cousins, so if you do upset them, a choccy treat could work wonders in making amends.

Gemini Goat

The Goat born under Gemini is a terrible worrier. These types seem to use their active minds to dream up all the troubles and problems that could result from every single action. Naturally, this renders decision-making almost impossible. They dither and rethink and ponder until finally someone else makes up their mind for them, at which point they are quite happy. In fact, if the Gemini Goat never had to make another decision, she would be a blissfully content creature.

Cancer Goat

Gentle, soft-hearted and kind, the Cancer Goat is a friend to all in need. These types would give their last penny to a homeless beggar in the street, and they always have a shoulder ready should anyone need to cry on it. Yet they can also be surprisingly moody for what appears to be no reason at all, and this characteristic can be baffling to their friends. No point in wasting time asking what's wrong, they find it difficult to explain. Just wait for the clouds to pass.

Leo Goat

The Leo Goat is a very fine specimen. Warm, friendly and more extrovert than her quieter Goat cousins, she seems to have the confidence other Goats often lack. Look more closely though, and you can find all is not quite as it seems. Frequently, that self-assured appearance is merely a well-presented 'front'. Back in the privacy of their own home, the bold Leo Goat can crumble. In truth, these types are easily hurt.

Virgo Goat

Outwardly vague and preoccupied, the Virgo Goat can turn unexpectedly fussy. These types are easy-going, but they can't stand messy homes, mud in their car or sweet wrappers lying around. Yet they would be genuinely surprised if anyone accused them of being pernickety. They believe they are laid back and good-humoured, which they are. Just don't drop chewing gum on their front path, that's all, and take your shoes off at the door.

Libra Goat

The Libra Goat is obliging to the point of self-sacrifice. These types are truly nice people. Generous with their time as well as their possessions. Unfortunately, their good nature is sometimes exploited by the unscrupulous. The Libra Goat will wear itself out in the service of those in distress, will refuse to hear a bad word about anyone and will remain loyal to friends despite the most intense provocation. The Libra Goat lives to please.

Scorpio Goat

Scorpio Goats are among the most strong-willed of all the Goats. They like to go their own way and hate to have others tell them what to do. They don't mind leaving irksome chores and duties to others, but woe betides anyone who tries to interfere with the Scorpio Goat's pet project. At first sight, they may appear preoccupied and have their heads in the clouds, but beneath that vague exterior, their sharp eyes miss very little. Don't underestimate the Scorpio Goat.

Sagittarius Goat

Sagittarius lends an adventurous streak to the normally cautious Goat make-up, and these types tend to take far more risks than their cousins born at other times of the year. While they still enjoy being taken care of, the Sagittarius Goat prefers cosseting on his return from adventures, not instead of them. These types are often good in business and amaze everyone by doing 'extremely well' apparently by accident.

Capricorn Goat

The Capricorn Goat, in contrast, is a very cautious creature. Danger beckons at every turn and security is top of their list of priorities. This Goat can never get to sleep until every door and window has been locked and secured. Should they find themselves staying in a hotel, Capricorn Goats will often drag a chair in front of the bedroom door, just in case. These types are difficult to get to know because it takes a while to win their trust, but once they become friends they will be loyal forever and despite their caution – or sensible outlook as they'd call it – they can be very successful.

Aquarius Goat

The Aquarius Goat tends to leap about from one high-minded project to the next. These well-meaning types might be manning a soup kitchen one day and devising a scheme to combat climate change the next. Their grand plans seldom come to fruition because they find the practical details so difficult to put into operation but should they link up with an organisational genius they could achieve great things.

Pisces Goat

The Pisces Goat is a very sensitive soul. These types are often highly gifted, and their best course of action is to find someone to take care of them as soon as possible so that they can get on with cultivating their talents. Left to themselves Pisces Goats will neglect their physical needs, failing to cook proper meals or dress warmly in cold weather. With the right guidance, however, they can work wonders.

Monkey

Aries Monkey

These cheeky types have a charm that is quite irresistible. Energetic and mischievous they adore parties and social gatherings of any kind. They crop up on every guest list because they are so entertaining. The Aries Monkey is a font of funny stories and silly jokes but seldom stands still for long. Friends of the Aries Monkey are often frustrated as their popular companion is so in demand it's difficult to pin her down for a catch-up.

Taurus Monkey

The Monkey born under the star sign of Taurus has a little more weight in his character. These types take life a shade more seriously than their delightfully frivolous cousins. Not that the Taurus Monkey is ever a stick-in-the-mud. It's just that business comes before pleasure with these types, although only just, and the business that catches their eye is not necessarily what others would call business. Taurus Monkey is as captivated by creating a useful container out of an old coffee jar as checking out a balance sheet.

Gemini Monkey

The Gemini Monkey Is a true comedian. Incredibly quick-witted, these types only have to open their mouths, and everyone around them is in stitches. If Oscar Wilde was not a Gemini Monkey, he should have been. People born under this sign could easily make a career in the comedy field if they can be bothered to make enough attempts. Truth is they're just as happy entertaining their friends as a theatre full of people.

Cancer Monkey

These types have a gentler side to their characters. Cancer Monkey's love to tinker with machinery and see how things work. They tend to take things to pieces and then forget to put them together again. They are easily hurt, however, if someone complains about this trait. They genuinely intend to put things right. It is just that somehow they never manage to get round to it, and they never realise that this is a trait they repeat over and over again.

Leo Monkey

The Leo Monkey is a highly adaptable creature. He can be all things to all men while still retaining his own unique personality. Popular, amusing and fond of practical jokes these types are welcome wherever they go. They can sometimes get rather carried away with the sound of their own voices and end up being rather tactless, but such is their charm that everyone forgives them. Occasionally, a practical joke can go too far, but kind-hearted Leo Monkey is horrified if anyone feels hurt, and instantly apologises.

Virgo Monkey

The Virgo Monkey could be a great inventor. The Monkey's natural ingenuity blends with Virgo's patience and fussiness over detail to create a character with the ideas to discover something new and the tenacity to carry on until it is perfected. If they could curb their impulse to rush on to the next brilliant idea when the last is complete, and turned their intention instead to marketing, they could make a fortune.

Libra Monkey

The Monkey born under the sign of Libra is actually a force to be reckoned with though no-one would ever guess it. These types are lovable and fun and have a knack of getting other people to do what they want without even realising they've been talked into it. In fact, Libran Monkeys are first-class manipulators but so skilled at their craft that nobody minds. These types could get away with murder.

Scorpio Monkey

Normally, the Monkey is a real chatterbox, but when Scorpio is added to the mix, you have a primate with the unusual gift of discretion right alongside his natural loquaciousness. These types will happily gossip all day long, but if they need to keep a secret, they are able to do so, to the grave if necessary. Scorpio Monkey could be an actor or a spy – and play each role to perfection. 007 could well have been a Scorpio Monkey.

Sagittarius Monkey

These flexible, amorous, adventure-loving Monkeys add zing to any gathering. These are the guests with the mad-cap ideas who want to jump fully clothed into the swimming pool at midnight and think it terrific fun to see in the New Year on top of Ben Nevis. It's difficult to keep up with the Sagittarius Monkey, but it's certainly fun to try.

Capricorn Monkey

Capricorn Monkeys have their serious side, but they are also flirty types. These are the subjects who charm with ease and tease and joke their conquests into bed. The trouble is Capricorn Monkey often promises more than is deliverable. These types tire more easily than they realise, and can't always put their exciting schemes into action. This rarely stops them trying, of course.

Aquarius Monkey

The Aquarius Monkey is a particularly inventive creature and employs his considerable intellect in trying to discover new ways to save the world. These types often have a hard time in their early years as it takes them decades to realise that not everyone sees the importance of their passions as they do. But, once they understand a different approach is needed, they go on to accomplish much in later life.

Pisces Monkey

The Pisces Monkey can be a puzzling creature. These types are dreamy and amusing one minute and irritable and quick-tempered the next. They can go with the flow so far and then suddenly wonder why no-one can keep up with them when they decide to get a move on. They tend to lack quite so much humour when the joke is on themselves, but most of the time they are agreeable companions.

Rooster

Aries Rooster

Stand well back when confronted with an Aries Rooster. These types are one hundred percent go-getter, and nothing will stand in their way. Aries Rooster can excel at anything to which he puts his mind, and as he frequently puts his mind to business matters, he's likely to end up a billionaire. Think scarlet sports cars, ostentatious homes, and a personal helicopter or two – the owner is bound to be an Aries Rooster.

Taurus Rooster

The Taurus Rooster has a heart of gold but can come over as a bit of a bossy boots, particularly in financial matters. These types believe they have a unique understanding of money and accounts and are forever trying to get more sloppy signs to sharpen up in this department. Even if their manner rankles, it's worth listening to their advice. Annoyingly, they are often right.

Gemini Rooster

The Rooster born under the sign of Gemini would make a terrific private detective were it not for the fact that Roosters find it almost impossible to blend into the background. Gemini Roosters love to find out what's going on and have an uncanny ability to stumble on the one thing you don't wish them to know. They mean no harm, however, and once they find a suitable outlet for their talents, they will go far.

Cancer Rooster

The Rooster born under the sign of Cancer is often a fine-looking creature and knows it. These types are secretly rather vain and behind the scenes take great pains with their appearance. They would die rather than admit it, however, and like to give the impression that their wonderful style is no more than a happy accident. Though they cultivate a relaxed, easy-going manner, a bad hair day or a splash of mud on their new suede boots is enough to send them into a major sulk for hours.

Leo Rooster

Not everyone takes to the Leo Rooster. The Lion is a naturally proud, extrovert sign and when allied to the strutting Rooster, there is a danger of these types ending up as bossy exhibitionists. Yet they really have the kindest of hearts and will leap from their pedestals in an instant to comfort someone who seems upset. A word of warning – they should avoid excessive alcohol as these types can get merry on a sniff of a cider apple.

Virgo Rooster

The Virgo Rooster is a hardworking, dedicated creature, devoted to family, but in an undemonstrative way. Wind this bird up at your peril, however. These types have little sense of humour when it comes to taking a joke, and they will hold a grudge for months if they feel someone has made them look foolish. They hate to be laughed at.

Libra Rooster

The Libra Rooster likes to look good, have a fine home and share his considerable assets with his closest friends. These types enjoy admiration, but they are more subtle than Leo Roosters and don't demand it quite so openly. Libra Rooster is quite happy to give but does expect gratitude in return.

Scorpio Rooster

The Scorpio Rooster is a heroic creature. These types will defend a position to the death. In days of old, many a Scorpio Rooster will have got involved in a duel because these types cannot endure insults, will fight aggression with aggression and will not back down under any circumstances. Foolhardy they may appear, but there is something admirable about them nevertheless.

Sagittarius Rooster

The Sagittarius Rooster tends to be a little excitable and rash. These types are bold and brash and ready for anything. They love to travel and are desperate to see what's over the next hill and around the next bend. Born explorers' they never want to tread the conventional travel path. Let others holiday in Marbella if they wish. Sagittarius Rooster prefers a walking tour of Tibet.

Capricorn Rooster

Capricorn brings a steadying quality to the impulsive Rooster. These types like to achieve, consolidate, and then build again. They believe they are amassing a fortune for their family and they usually do. However, sometimes, their families would prefer a little less security and more attention. Best not to mention it to Capricorn Rooster though – this Rooster is likely to feel hurt and offended.

Aquarius Rooster

The Aquarius Rooster is frequently misunderstood. These types mean well but they tend to be impulsive and speak before they think, accidentally offending others when they do so. In fact, the Aquarius Rooster is a sensitive creature beneath that brash exterior and is easily hurt. If they can learn to count to ten before saying anything controversial, and maybe rephrase, they'd be amazed at how successful they'd become.

Pisces Rooster

The Pisces Rooster has a secret fear. He is terrified that one day he will be terribly poor. These types save hard to stave off that dreadful fate and will only feel totally relaxed when they have a huge nest egg behind them. Despite this, they manage to fall in and out of love regularly and often end up delighting their partners with the wonderful lifestyle they can create.

Dog

Aries Dog

The Aries Dog is a friendly type. Extrovert and sociable these subjects like a lively career and cheerful home life. They are not excessively materialistic, but they tend to make headway in the world without trying too hard. Aries Dog likes to get things done and will bound from one task to the next with energy and enthusiasm.

Taurus Dog

The Dog born under the star sign of Taurus is the most dependable creature in the world. Their word really is their bond, and they will never break a promise while there is breath in their body. They tend to be ultra-conservative with a small 'c'. The men are inclined to be chauvinists, and the women usually hold traditional views. They really do prefer to make their home and family their priority. They are loyal and kind, and people instinctively trust them.

Gemini Dog

The Gemini Dog, in contrast, while never actually dishonest, can be a bit of a sly fox when necessary. The quickest of all Dogs, the Gemini breed gets impatient when the going gets slow and resorts to the odd trick to speed things along. Nevertheless, these types are truthful and honest in their own way and have a knack of falling on their feet… whatever happens.

Cancer Dog

The Cancer Dog was born to be in a settled relationship. These types are never totally happy until they've found their true love and built a cosy home to snuggle up in together. Cancer Dog is not overly concerned with a career. As long as these types earn enough to pay the mortgage and buy life's essentials, they are happy. The right companionship is what they crave. With the perfect partner by their side, they are truly content.

Leo Dog

If Leo Dogs really did have four legs, chances are they would be police dogs. These types are sticklers for law and order. They will not tolerate injustice and will seek out wrongdoers and plague them until they change their ways. Woe betide any workmate who is pilfering pens, making free with office coffee or fiddling expenses. The Leo Dog will force them to own up and make amends. Should you be a victim of injustice, however, Leo Dog will zoom to your aid.

Virgo Dog

The Virgo Dog tends to be a great worrier. A born perfectionist, Virgo Dog agonises over every detail and loses sleep if he suspects he has performed any task badly. These types are very clever and can achieve great things, but too often they fail to enjoy their success because they are too busy worrying they might have made a mistake. The crazy thing is, they very seldom do.

Libra Dog

The Libra Dog believes in 'live and let live'. A laid back, tolerant fellow, Libra Dog likes to lie in the sun and not interfere with anyone. Let sleeping dogs lie is definitely her motto. She will agree to almost anything for a quiet life. Yet it's unwise to push her too far. When there's no alternative, this particular hound can produce a very loud bark.

Scorpio Dog

The Scorpio Dog is as loyal and trustworthy as other canines, but more difficult to get to know. Beneath that amiable exterior is a very suspicious heart. These types don't quite understand why they are so wary of others, but it takes them a long time to learn to trust. Perhaps they are afraid of getting hurt. The idea of marriage fills them with terror, and it takes a very patient partner to get them to the altar. Once married, however, they will be faithful and true.

Sagittarius Dog

The Sagittarius Dog is inexhaustible. These cheerful types are always raring to go and quite happy to join in with any adventure. They love to be part of the gang and are perfectly willing to follow someone else's lead. They don't mind if their ideas are not always accepted; they just like being involved. These types work splendidly in teams and can achieve great things in a group.

Capricorn Dog

The Capricorn Dog is a very caring type. These subjects are happy so long as their loved ones are happy, but they greatly fear that a friend or family member might fall ill. This concern, probably kept secret, gives them real anxiety and should a loved one show worrying symptoms, the Capricorn Dog will suffer sleepless nights until the problem is resolved. When they are not urging their families to keep warm and put on an extra vest, these types are likely to be out and about helping others less fortunate than themselves.

Aquarius Dog

The Aquarius Dog, when young, spends a great deal of time searching for a worthy cause to which they can become devoted. Since there are so many worthy causes from which to choose these types can suffer much heartache as they struggle to pick the right one. When – at last –

a niche is found, however, the Aquarius Dog will settle down to a truly contented life of quiet satisfaction. These types need to serve and feel that they are improving life for others. This is their path to happiness.

Pisces Dog

Like the Aquarius breed, the Pisces Dog often has a number of false starts early in life although these are more likely to be of a romantic rather than philanthropic nature. The Pisces Dog wants to find a soulmate but is not averse to exploring a few cul-de-sacs on the way. These types are not promiscuous, however, and when they do find Mr or Miss Right, they are blissfully happy to settle down.

Pig

Aries Pig

The Aries Pig always seems to wear a smile on its face and no wonder. Everything seems to go right for these cheerful types, and they scarcely seem to have to lift a finger to make things fall perfectly into place. In fact, of course, their good luck is the result of sheer hard work, but the Aries Pig has a knack of making work look like play so that nobody realises the effort Pig is putting in.

Taurus Pig

Most Pigs are happy, but the Taurus Pigs really seem quite blissful most of the time. One of their favourite occupations is eating, and they delight in dreaming up sumptuous menus and then creating them for the enjoyment of themselves and their friends. For this reason, Taurus Pigs have a tendency to put on weight. Despite the time they devote to their hobby, however, Taurus Pigs usually do well in their career. Many gifted designers are born under this sign.

Gemini Pig

The Gemini Pig has a brilliant business brain gift-wrapped in a charming, happy go lucky personality. These types usually zoom straight to the top of their chosen tree, but they manage to do so smoothly and easily without ruffling too many feathers on the way. They are popular with their workmates, and later their employees, and nobody can figure out how quite such a nice, down to earth type has ended up in such a position of authority.

Cancer Pig

The Cancer Pig likes to give the impression of being a very hard working type. She is hard working, of course, but perhaps not quite as excessively as she likes others to believe. Secretly, the Cancer Pig makes sure there's plenty of time to spare for fun and indulgence. To the outside world, however, Pig pretends to be constantly slaving away and likes to get regular appreciation for these efforts.

Leo Pig

The Leo Pig is delightful company. Friendly, amusing and very warm and approachable. These types do however have a tremendously lazy streak. Left to themselves, they would not rise till noon, and they prefer someone else to do all the cleaning and cooking. The Leo Pig has to be nagged to make an effort, but when these types do so, they can achieve impressive results.

Virgo Pig

The Virgo Pig, in contrast, is a highly conscientious creature. These types can't abide laziness, and while they are normally kindly, helpful souls who gladly assist others, they will not lift a finger to aid someone who has brought his problems on himself through slovenliness. The Virgo Pig is a clean, contented type who usually achieves a happy life.

Libra Pig

The creative Libra Pig is always dreaming up new ways to improve their home. These types love to be surrounded by beautiful and comfortable things but seldom get round to completing their ideas because they are having such a good time in other ways. This is probably just as well because the minute they decide on one colour scheme, they suddenly see something that might work better. A permanent work in progress is probably the best option.

Scorpio Pig

The Scorpio Pig usually goes far. The amiable Pig boosted by powerful, almost psychic Scorpio can seem turbo-charged at times. These types keep their own counsel more than their chatty cousins, and this often stands them in good stead in business. They can be a little too cautious at times, but they rarely make mistakes.

Sagittarius Pig

Eat, drink and be merry is the motto of the Sagittarius Pig. These types have the intelligence to go far in their careers but, in truth, they would rather party. They love to dress up, get together with a bunch of friends and laugh and dance until dawn. Sagittarius Pig hates to be alone for long, so is always off in search of company.

Capricorn Pig

Pigs are normally broad-minded types, but the Capricorn Pig is a little more staid than his cousins. Nevertheless, being able to narrow their vision gives these types the ability to channel their concentration totally onto the subject in hand, a gift which is vital to success in many professions. For this reason, Capricorn Pigs often make a name for themselves in their chosen career.

Aquarius Pig

Honest, straightforward and popular Aquarius Pigs have more friends than they can count. Always good-humoured and cheerful these types gravitate to those in need and do whatever they can to help. The Aquarius Pig gives copiously to charity and frequently wishes to do more. These types tend to have their heads in the clouds most of the time and for this reason, tend not to give their careers or finances the attention they should. But since worldly success means little to the Aquarius Pig, this hardly matters.

Pisces Pig

The Pisces Pig is a particularly sweet-natured creature. These types are real dreamers. They float around in a world of their own, and people tend to make allowances for them. Yet, from time to time, the Pisces Pig drifts in from his other planet to startle everyone with a stunningly brilliant idea. There is more to the Pisces Pig than meets the eye.

Rat

Aries Rat

Fiery Aries adds more than usual urgency to the sociable Rat. While these types enjoy company, they also tend to be impatient and can get quite bad-tempered and aggressive with anyone who seems to waste their time. Aries Rats do not suffer fools and will stomp off on their own if someone annoys them. In fact, this is the best thing all round. Aries Rats hate to admit it, but they benefit from a little solitude which enables them to calm down and recharge their batteries. Happily, as quickly as these types flare up, they just as quickly cool off again.

Taurus Rat

When Taurus, renowned for a love of luxury and the finer things in life, is born in a comfort-loving Rat year, a true gourmet and bon viveur has entered the world. The Taurus effect enhances the sensuous parts of the Rat personality and lifts them to new heights. Good food is absolutely essential to these types. They don't eat to live; they really do live to eat. Many excellent chefs are born under this sign, and even those folks who don't make catering their career are likely to be outstanding home cooks. Dinner parties thrown by Taurus Rats are memorable affairs. The only drawback with these types is that they can become a little pernickety and overly fussy about details. They also have to watch their weight.

Gemini Rat

While Taurus accentuates the Rat's love of good living, Gemini heightens the Rat's already well-developed social skills. That crowd chuckling and laughing around the witty type in the corner are bound to be listening to a Gemini Rat. Amusing, quick-thinking, and never lost for words, the only things likely to drive Gemini Rats away are bores and undue seriousness. Gemini Rats prefer light, entertaining conversation and head for the hills when things get too heavy. Delightful as they always are however, it is difficult to capture the attention of a Gemini Rat for long. These types love to circulate. They make an entrance and then move on to pastures new. Pinning them down never works. They simply lose interest and with it that famous sparkle.

Cancer Rat

Cancer makes the Rat a little more sensitive and easily hurt than usual. These types are emotional and loving but sometimes come across as martyrs. They work hard but tend to feel, often without good cause, their efforts are not as well appreciated as they should be. Cancer Rats frequently suspect they are being taken for granted at home and at work, but their love of company prevents them from making too big a fuss. Rats are naturally gifted business people, and the Cancer Rat has a particularly good head for financial affairs. These types enjoy working with others, and they are especially well suited to partnerships. However, don't expect the sensitive, feeling Cancer Rat to be a pushover. These types can be surprisingly demanding at work and will not tolerate any laziness on the part of employees.

Leo Rat

Leo Rats usually get to the top. Few people can resist them. The combination of Rat sociability, business acumen and ambition, coupled with extrovert Leo's rather, shall we say, 'pushy', qualities and flair for leadership can't help but power these types to the top of whatever tree they happen to choose to climb. Along the way, however, they may irritate those few less gifted souls who fail to fall under their spell. Such doubters may complain that Leo Rat hogs the limelight and tends to become overbearing at times but since hardly anyone else seems to notice, why should Leo Rat care?

Virgo Rat

As we have already seen, the delightful Rat does have a stingy streak in his make-up, and when the astrological sign of Virgo is added to the mix, this characteristic tends to widen. At best, Virgo Rats are terrific savers and do wonders with their investments. The Rat tendency to squander money on unwise bargains is almost entirely absent in these types, and they often end up seriously rich. At worst, however, in negative types, Virgo Rats can be real Scrooges, grating the last sliver of soap to save on washing powder, sitting in the dark to conserve electricity and attempting their own shoe repairs with stick-on soles, even when they have plenty of money in the bank. Virgo Rats are brilliant at detail; but in negative types, they put this gift to poor use spending far too long on money-saving schemes when they would do much better to look for ways of expanding their income.

Libra Rat

The Libra Rat adores company even more than most. In fact, these types are seldom alone. They have dozens of friends, their phones never stop ringing, and most evenings the Libra Rat is entertaining. Libra Rat enjoys civilised gatherings rather than wild parties and friends will be treated to beautiful music, exquisite food and a supremely comfortable home. These types really can charm the birds off the trees, not with the brilliant repartee of the Gemini Rat but with a warmth and low key humour all their own. These types do tend to be a touch lazier than the usual Rat and their weakness for bargains, particularly in the areas of art and fashion, is more pronounced, but their charm is so strong that partners forgive them for overspending.

Scorpio Rat

It's often said that Rats would make good journalists or detectives because beneath that expansive surface is a highly observant brain. Well the best of them all would be the Rat born under Scorpio. A veritable Sherlock Holmes of a Rat if you wish to be flattering, or a real nosey parker if you don't. These types are endlessly curious. They want to know everything that's going on, who is doing what with whom where and for how long. They may not have any particular use for the information they gather, but they just can't help gathering it all the same. Scorpio Rats often have psychic powers though they may not be aware of this and these powers aid them in their 'research'. Unlike other Rats, those born under Scorpio prefer their own company and like to work alone. When they manage to combine their curiosity and talent for digging out information, there is almost no limit to what they can achieve with their career

Sagittarius Rat

Traditionally Rats have many friends, but the Sagittarius Rat has the not so welcome distinction of collecting a few enemies along the way as well. The Sagittarius Rat finds this quite extraordinary as he never intends to upset anyone. It's just that these types can be forthright to the point of rudeness and an affable nature can only compensate so far. These types are amicable and warm, but when they speak their minds, some people never forgive them. Despite this tendency, Sagittarius Rats have a knack for accumulating money and plough it back into their business to good effect. They manage to be generous, and a bit mean at the same time, which baffles their friends, but those that have not been offended by Sagittarius Rat's tactless tongue tend to stay loyal forever.

Capricorn Rat

Rats are naturally high achievers, but perhaps the highest achiever of them all is likely to be born under the sign of Capricorn. These types are not loud and brilliant like Leo Rats. They tend to be quietly ambitious. They keep in the background, watching what needs to be done, astutely judging who counts and who does not, and then when they are absolutely sure they are on solid ground, they move in. After such preparation, they are unlikely to make a mistake, but if they do they blame themselves, they are bitterly angry, and they resolve never to repeat their stupidity. Reckless these types are not, but their methods produce good results, and they make steady progress towards their goals.

Aquarius Rat

All Rats are blessed with good brains, but few of them think of themselves as intellectuals. The exceptions are the Rats born under the sign of Aquarius. While being friendly and sociable, the Aquarian Rat also needs time alone to think things through and to study the latest subject that has aroused his interest. Perhaps not so adept at business as most Rats, those born under the sign of Aquarius make up for any deficiency in this department by teeming with good ideas. They are intuitive, very hard working and love to be involved in 'people' projects.

Pisces Rat

Pisces Rats tend to be quieter than their more flamboyant brothers and sisters. They are not drawn to the limelight, and they are not so interested in business as other Rats. In fact, working for other people has little appeal for them, although this is what they often end up doing through want of thinking up a better idea. Should a more enterprising Pisces Rat decide to put his mind to business, however, he will often end up self-employed which suits him extremely well. Having taken the plunge, many a self-employed Pisces Rat surprises himself by doing very well indeed. These types can be amazingly shrewd and intuitive, and once these powers are harnessed to the right career, they progress in leaps and bounds. Pisces Rats tend to do well in spite of themselves.

Ox

Aries Ox

Dynamic Aries brings the Ox a very welcome blast of fire and urgency to stir those methodical bones into faster action. This is a fortunate combination because when the steadfast, industrious, patient qualities of the Ox are combined with quickness of mind and a definite purpose, very little can stand in the way of this subject's progress. Aries Oxen do particularly well in careers where enormous discipline combined with flair and intelligence is required. Many writers are born under this sign as are college lecturers, historical researchers and archaeologists.

Taurus Ox

Oxen are notoriously stubborn creatures but combine them with Taurus the bull and this trait is doubled if not quadrupled. It is not a good idea to box these types into a corner because they will take a stand and refuse to budge even if the house is on fire. Taurean Oxen really will cut off their noses to spite their faces if they feel they have to. Fall out with them and stop talking, and the chances are that the feud will continue to the grave. Yet despite this tendency, Oxen born under the sign of Taurus are not unfriendly types. They are utterly reliable and totally loyal. Family and friends trust them completely. They might be a bit old fashioned and inflexible, but they are lovable too.

Gemini Ox

Chatty Gemini transforms the normally taciturn Ox into a beast which is almost loquacious, at least by the normal standards of these strong silent types. They might even be confident enough to attempt a few jokes, and though humour is not the Oxen's strongpoint, the Gemini Ox can usually produce something respectably amusing if not sidesplittingly funny. Oddly enough, should the Ox set his mind to it and apply his awesome hard work and patience to the subject of humour he might even make a career of it. Some Gemini Oxen have even become accomplished comedians – not simply through natural talent but through sheer hard work and perseverance. More frequently, however, the combination of Gemini with the Ox produces a 'poor man's lawyer' – a highly opinionated individual who can see what's wrong with the government and the legal system and loves to put the world to rights at every opportunity.

Cancer Ox

Oxen born under the sign of Cancer can go very far indeed, not through the application of brainpower although they are by no means unintelligent, but through the skills they have at their fingertips. These subjects are the craftsmen of the universe. Diligent, painstaking, and precise, they are incapable of bodging any practical task they undertake. They will spend hours and hours honing whatever craft has taken their fancy until they reach what looks to others like the peak of perfection. The Cancer Ox won't accept this of course. He can detect the minutest flaw in his own handiwork, but when he is finally forced to hand it over, everyone else is delighted with his efforts. Many artists, potters and sculptors are born under this sign.

Leo Ox

When the Lion of Leo meets the enormous strength of the Ox, the result is a formidable individual, indeed. Annoy or mock these powerful types at your peril. And anyone who dares to pick a fight with the Lion-Ox is likely to come out of it very badly. Most of the time, however, Leo is a friendly lion bringing confidence and a more relaxed attitude to the unbending Ox. These types are more broad-minded and open-hearted than the usual Oxen. They have been known to enjoy parties and once tempted into the limelight they may even find it's not as bad as they feared. In fact, secretly, they're having a ball.

Virgo Ox

Oxen born under the sign of Virgo tend to be very caring types. Though they show their feelings in practical ways and shun sloppy, emotional displays you can rely on an Ox born under Virgo to comfort the sick, help the old folk and notice if anyone in the neighbourhood needs assistance. Florence Nightingale could have been a Virgo Ox. The unsentimental but immensely useful and humane work she did for her sick soldiers is typical of these types. They make excellent nurses and careworkers, forever plumping pillows, smoothing sheets and knowing just the right touches to bring comfort where it is needed. On a personal level, these subjects are inclined to be critical and easily irritated by the small failings of others, but their bark is worse than their bite. Their kindness shines through.

Libra Ox

Generally speaking the down to earth Ox has little time for putting on the charm. As far as Ox is concerned, people either like you or they don't, and it's not worth worrying about it either way. There's no point in wasting valuable time trying to bend your personality to accommodate the whims of others. Yet when the Ox is born under the sign of Libra, this trait is modified somewhat. Libra people just can't help having charm even if they are Oxen and therefore express that charm more brusquely than usual. The Libran Ox glides effortlessly through life, pleasing others without even realising it. These types are sympathetic and like to help those in need wherever possible. Try to take advantage of their good nature or trick them with an untrue sob story, though, and they will never forgive you.

Scorpio Ox

The typical Ox is notoriously difficult to get to know, and when that Ox happens to be born under the secretive sign of Scorpio, you might as well give up and go home. You'll learn nothing from this creature unless he has some special reason for telling you. Stubborn and silent, these types are very deep indeed; they care nothing for the opinions of others and follow their own impenetrable hearts come what may. However, win the love of one of these unique subjects, and you have a very rare prize indeed. You will unlock a devotion and passion that you have probably never experienced before and will probably never experience again. This is a strangely compelling combination.

Sagittarius Ox

The Ox born under Sagittarius is a more carefree type than his brothers and sisters. Something of the free spirit of the horse touches these subjects, and while there is no chance of them kicking up their heels or doing anything remotely irresponsible, they at least understand these temptations in others and take a more relaxed view of life. The Ox born under Sagittarius is ambitious but independent. These types don't like to be told what to do and are probably more suited to being self-employed than working for others. They are more easy-going than a lot of Oxen and for this reason attract a wider range of friends. Like their Gemini cousins, they might even hazard a joke from time to time. All in all, the Ox born under Sagittarius gets more fun out of life.

Capricorn Ox

Unlike his Sagittarian brother, the Ox born under Capricorn takes himself and life very seriously indeed. These types usually do very well in material terms and often end up in positions of authority; yet if they're not careful, they can look burned out. With good reason. Capricorn Oxen have never learned how to relax, and they see life as a struggle; consequently, for them, it is. Yet they have much to be glad for. They are great savers for a rainy day, and so they never have to worry about unpaid bills, their capacity for hard work is so enormous they can hardly help but achieve a great deal, and before very long they find themselves well off and regarded with respect by everyone in the community. If these types could only manage to unwind, be gentle with themselves and enjoy their success, they could be very happy indeed.

Aquarius Ox

The Ox has never been a flashy sign. These types believe actions speak louder than words, and they like to beaver away without drawing attention to themselves. When this trait is coupled with the slightly introverted though idealistic nature of Aquarius, you get a quiet, complex character who prefers to work behind the scenes and turns modest when the limelight is switched on. Never known for his verbal dexterity, the Ox born under Aquarius can suddenly turn into a persuasive orator when a humanitarian cause sparks unexpected passion. These types make loyal, faithful companions to those who take the trouble to understand them and their intelligence and dogged persistence makes them invaluable as researchers, political assistants and private secretaries.

Pisces Ox

Few Oxen can be described as fey, changeable creatures but those that come the closest will be found under the sign of Pisces. Pisces brings an emotional, artistic quality to the steadfast Ox. These types are loving, faithful and true, yet it is often difficult to guess what they are thinking. Of all the Ox family, Pisces Oxen are likely to be the most moody and yet in many ways also the most creative. The Ox input lends strength and stamina to more delicate Pisces constitutions, enabling them to accomplish far more than other Pisces subjects. Just leave them alone until they're ready to face the world.

Tiger

Aries Tiger

Another combination which could be potentially explosive but in this case, energetic Aries adds force and power to the Tiger's humanitarian instincts while the Tiger's unworldly nature curbs Aries materialistic streak. These types really could change the world for the better if they put their minds to it. They are kind and thoughtful, and while they might be impatient at times, they quickly regret any harsh words spoken in the heat of the moment.

Taurus Tiger

Taurus Tigers are tremendous achievers. The strength of the zodiac bull added to the fire of the Tiger produces a truly formidable individual who can do almost anything to which he sets his mind. These types often end up making a great deal of money. They have to work hard for all their gains, but this doesn't worry them at all. They also take a great deal of pleasure in spending their hard-earned cash. They like to share what they've got, and this gives them such childish joy that no-one begrudges them their good fortune.

Gemini Tiger

The quicksilver mind of Gemini adds zing and extra flexibility to the Tiger's powerful individualism. These Tigers are blessed with minds which overflow with brilliant ideas. They are creative and often artistic too, so they're capable of wonderful achievements. Their only drawback is that they possess almost too much of a good thing. They have so many ideas that they tend to zoom off at a tangent onto a new task before they have completed the one on which they were working.

Cancer Tiger

These Tigers are immensely clever but a little more retiring than the usual bold, brave terror of the jungle. No Tiger is timid, but Cancer has the effect of quietening the more reckless excesses of the Tiger and allowing a little caution to creep into the blend. They still like a challenge but will opt for something a little less physically demanding than other Tigers. These types are more able to fit into society and tolerate authority better than other Tigers, and for this reason they often do well in their careers.

Leo Tiger

What would you get if you crossed a lion with a tiger? A very wild beast indeed. Some sort of striped wonder of the world no doubt! Leo Tigers certainly make their mark. Tigers are big, beautiful, fearless personalities who crave the limelight and love to be noticed. They believe in doing good deeds, but they like to be noticed doing them. These are not the types of which anonymous benefactors are made. When the Leo Tiger raises money for charity, he likes to make sure the world's press are gathered to record the occasion if at all possible. Yet his heart's in the right place. Let these Tigers have their share of praise, and they will work wonders for others.

Virgo Tiger

The Virgo Tiger is quite a different beast. Virgo accentuates the Tiger's already well-developed sense of justice. These types cannot rest until wrongdoers have got their just deserts. They often go into professions involving the law and the police force. They are immensely self-disciplined and have very high standards. Totally trustworthy and effective, they can sometimes be a little difficult to live with. They are not unkind; it's just that they expect everyone else to be as perfect as they are themselves. Yet Virgo adds attention-to-detail to Tiger's passion to change the world, and the combination creates a character who really could make a lasting difference.

Libra Tiger

Laidback Libra brings quite a different quality to the Tiger. Tiger's intensity is softened by pure Libra charm, and the result is a Tiger of unrivalled compassion and magnetism. Libra Tigers often end up in the caring professions where people flock to them with relief. These Tigers want to help, and Libra gives them the ability to understand just what people need and when. You'd never catch a Libra Tiger helping an old lady across the road who didn't wish to go. Libra Tiger would realise at once that the woman was waiting for a bus, would stand with her to keep her company, help her on when the vehicle arrived and make sure the driver put her off at the right stop. No wonder these Tigers are so well-loved wherever they go.

Scorpio Tiger

Crossing a Scorpion with a Tiger is a very tricky proposition. These types mean well, but they are often misunderstood. Scorpio brings a tremendous depth of feeling to the Tiger's reforming instincts, but this sometimes causes them to put tremendous effort into the wrong causes with alarming results. These types can be very quick-tempered, and they may nurse a grudge for a long time. They never forgive disloyalty, and they never forget. It would be a serious mistake to make an enemy of a Scorpio Tiger – but once this individual becomes a friend, they'll be loyal for life.

Sagittarius Tiger

Another charmer, the Sagittarius Tiger is nevertheless likely to hit the road at the slightest opportunity. These types are wanderers, and no matter how much they seem to enjoy company, they enjoy moving on even more. They can't bear working for other people and do far better being self-employed. The travel industry would suit them perfectly. Impossible to cage in or pin down – don't even try – the only way to have a happy relationship with a Sagittarius Tiger is to make them feel free at all times.

Capricorn Tiger

Steady Capricorn lends a prudent touch to the impulsive Tiger, and these types are the Tigers most likely to stop and think before rushing off to save the rain forest. They still enjoy improving the world, but they check travel arrangements, make sure they have got sufficient funds and do a bit of research online first. These are not party animals. While they enjoy company, they prefer serious discussion to frivolous small talk and much as they enjoy travel they appreciate the comfort of home. These Tigers like to develop their theories from the depths of their favourite armchair beside their own cosy hearth.

Aquarius Tiger

When idealistic Aquarius meets idealistic Tiger, you have to hang onto that long tiger tail to keep these subjects, feet on the ground. These types really do have their heads in the clouds and are totally unpredictable. Once a worthwhile cause presents itself, they will rush off immediately without a thought to the consequences. Convention is of no interest to them. They couldn't care less what other people think. They go through life guided entirely by a strong inner sense of right and wrong. If it's right, they know it without a shadow of a doubt; if it's wrong, they will not do it no matter what anyone says. This attitude can get them into a lot of trouble, but other signs sneakily admire their courage. People may not agree with Aquarius Tiger, but no one can doubt his integrity.

Pisces Tiger

One of Tiger's failings is a tendency to be indecisive without warning, and this trait is heightened in Pisces Tigers. These types are anxious to do the right thing; it's just that sometimes it's very difficult to know what that right thing is. There are so many alternatives. Pisces Tiger is kind and gentle and apt to get sentimental at times. They want to save the world, but they'd like someone alongside to help them – though not too many. Despite their indecision, they usually end up heading in the right direction in the end. Yet, even when they've achieved a great deal, they still agonise over whether they could have done even more.

CHAPTER 17: CREATE A WONDERFUL YEAR

By now, you should have got a pretty good idea of the main influences on your life and personality, according to Chinese astrology. But how is 2023 going to shape up for you? Well, that largely depends on how cleverly you play your hand.

Rabbit years are traditionally regarded as happy and harmonious. There are changes, of course, as there are every year, but in general the changes are mild and predictable. There should be far fewer shocks than we experience in a Tiger year.

The key point is that – according to Chinese astrology – everything should be in balance. So, after the hectic, drastic energy that ripped through last year's Year of the Tiger, the world is desperate for a respite. A pause to reflect, relax, and rebuild; to restore the planet's balance. After 12 months of tearing things down to build back better, we're ready for some time out, to rest, recuperate, and assemble the building materials we'll need to create the new structures.

In 2023, the emphasis will be on people power, diplomacy, and solving disagreements with dialogue.

Some signs will find these conditions more comfortable than others. Zodiac creatures that prefer to keep things as they are – those that tend to err on the side of caution and who like to reflect long and hard before making changes – will find 2023 a huge relief after the uncertainties of last year. Energetic, always-on-the-go types, however, could find the proceedings a little dull – though the renaissance in entertainment might perk things up for them. But, whichever group you belong to, as long as you're prepared – and you know what you might be up against – you can develop a strategy to ride those waves like a world-class surfer.

Sit back and rely on good fortune alone, because it's a terrific year for your sign, and you could snatch failure from the jaws of success. Navigate any stormy seas with skill and foresight, if it's not such a sunny year for your sign, and you'll sail on to fulfil your dreams. This is always true *in any year*, but doubly so when the resourceful Rabbit is in charge. Above all, the Rabbit supports kindness, consideration, modesty and family values. So, no matter what zodiac sign you were born under, 'Rabbit year energy' will help you… if you help yourself.

The future is not set in stone.

Chinese astrology is used very much like a weather forecast, so that you can check out the likely conditions you'll encounter on your journey and plan your route and equipment accordingly. Some signs might need a parasol and sandals; while others require stout walking boots and rain gear. Yet, properly prepared, both will end up in a good place at the end of the trip.

Finally, it's said that if you feel another sign has a much better outlook than you this year, you can carry a small symbol of that animal with you (in the form of a piece of jewellery, perhaps, or a tiny charm in your pocket or bag) and their good luck will rub off on you. Does it work? For some, maybe, but there's certainly no harm in trying.

Other Books from the Publisher

Linda Dearsley – *the author of this book* – was Doris Stokes' ghost.

Well, more accurately, she was the ghost-writer for Doris Stokes and worked with her for 10 years to produce 7 books, detailing the great lady's life.

In Voices Everywhere, Linda shines a light on her time working with Doris, right from the very early days when Doris was doing private readings in her Fulham flat, to filling the London Palladium and Barbican night after night, to subsequent fame outside the UK. Throughout all this, Doris Stokes never became anyone other than who she was: a kind, generous, and down-to-earth woman with an extraordinary gift, and a fondness for a nice cup of tea. January 6th, 2020, would have been Doris' 100th birthday.

Following Doris' death, Linda chronicles how cynics tried to torpedo the Stokes legacy with accusations of cheating and dishonesty, but how those closest to Doris never believed she was anything other than genuine.

In turn, as the months and years rolled by, more and more intriguing people crossed Linda's path, each with their own unexplainable power, and Doris never seemed far away. From the palmist who saw pictures in people's hands, to the couple whose marriage was predicted by Doris, and the woman who believes she captures departed spirits on camera – the mysterious world of the paranormal, and Doris Stokes' place within it, continues to unfold.

Karina Collins is an acclaimed Tarot reader who has helped people, from all walks of life, to better understand their lives' journeys.

Now, she is on a mission to help you take control of your life — through the power of Tarot — to better explore and understand your purpose and destiny.

Do you have questions about now and your future? Perhaps about making more money, or whether love is on the horizon, or whether you will become happier? Do you want to steer your life in a direction that brings success, pleasure, and fulfilment? Well, Tarot is a means to help you do exactly that! Used for centuries, it provides a powerful tool for unlocking knowledge, divining the future, and delivering shortcuts to the lives we desire.

In this full-colour book, Karina provides explanations and insights into the full 78-card Tarot deck, how to phrase questions most effectively, real-world sample readings, why seemingly scary cards represent opportunities for growth and triumph, and more.

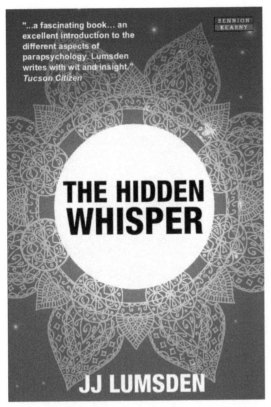

"...a fascinating book... an excellent introduction to the different aspects of parapsychology. Lumsden writes with wit and insight."
Tucson Citizen

BENNION KEARNY

THE HIDDEN WHISPER

JJ LUMSDEN

A paranormal puzzle smoulders in the desert heat of southern Arizona. At the home of Jack and Chloe Monroe, a written message "Leave Now" appears then disappears, a candle in an empty room mysteriously lights itself, and – most enigmatically – an unidentifiable ethereal whisper begins to permeate the house. What was once simply strange now feels sinister. What once seemed a curiosity now seems terrifying.

Dr. Luke Jackson, a British Parapsychologist visiting family nearby, is asked to investigate and quickly finds himself drawn deeper into the series of unexplained events. Time is against him. He has just one week to understand and resolve the poltergeist case before he must depart Arizona.

The Hidden Whisper is the acclaimed paranormal thriller, written by real-life parapsychologist Dr. JJ Lumsden, which offers a rare opportunity to enter the intriguing world of parapsychology through the eyes of Luke Jackson. The fictional narrative is combined with extensive endnotes and references that cover Extra Sensory Perception, Psychokinesis, Haunts, Poltergeists, Out of Body Experiences, and more. If you thought parapsychology was like Ghostbusters – think again...

"This book works on many levels, an excellent introduction to the concepts current in the field of parapsychology... at best you may learn something new, and at worst you'll have read a witty and well-written paranormal detective story" Parascience.

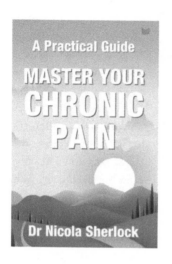

A Practical Guide

MASTER YOUR
CHRONIC
PAIN

Dr Nicola Sherlock

SPEND GREEN AND
SAVE THE WORLD

Tackling Climate Change Through The
Consumer-Led Movement

LIZ CHRISTOU

THE
15
Minute
RULE
for
FORGIVENESS

CAROLINE BUCHANAN

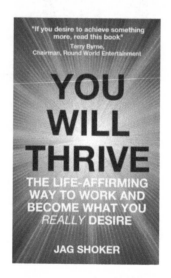

"If you desire to achieve something
more, read this book"
Terry Byrne,
Chairman, Round World Entertainment

YOU
WILL
THRIVE

THE LIFE-AFFIRMING
WAY TO WORK AND
BECOME WHAT YOU
REALLY DESIRE

JAG SHOKER

Lightning Source UK Ltd.
Milton Keynes UK
UKHW011318130123
415295UK00005B/422